THE SHIFT FROM

FROM

ME TO *TEAM*

Unleashing Sustainable Greatness

Also by Fritz Seyferth

The Heart of a Champion, 2008
(with Glenn "Bo" Schembechler and Kim A. Eagle, M.D.)

THE SHIFT
FROM
ME TO *TEAM*

Unleashing Sustainable Greatness

FRITZ SEYFERTH

FS/A Press

FS/A Press
600 S. Wagner
Ann Arbor, MI 48103
(734) 332-8020 | teamfsa@team-fsa.com | https://team-fsa.com/

LIBRARY OF CONGRESS CATALOGING-IN-PUBLICATION DATA
Seyferth, Fritz
The shift from me to we : unleashing sustainable success / Fritz Seyferth.
Includes index.
LCCN 2023903247 (print) |
ISBN 979-8-9875638-0-9 (paperback) | ISBN 979-8-9875638-1-6 (ebook) |
ISBN 979-8-9875638-2-3 (audiobook) |

Printed in the United States of America

Project Manager and Copy Editor: Janet Max
Cover Design: Phire Group
Interior Graphics: Phire Group and Janet Max

For more information about *The Shift from Me to We*, FS/A, and Fritz Seyferth

DEDICATION

This book is dedicated to my wife, Lynn, and to the amazing three children she raised, to our twelve grandchildren, who I hope will live thriving lives of contribution, to my mom and dad—Jack and Corrie—who showed us how to live life to the fullest, and to my mentor Bo Schembechler, who was a best friend, father figure, and confidant much of my life. Thank you.

TABLE OF CONTENTS

FOREWORD . . . . **xix**

PREFACE . . . . **xxi**

ACKNOWLEDGMENTS . . . .**xxiii**

THE PROBLEM WE ADDRESS 1

    The Decline in Employee Engagement 1

    The Team Is Struggling 1

INTRODUCTION 5

    The State of Flow 5

    The Enablers of Sustainable Greatness 8

    The Leadership Shift from *Me* to *Team* 8

    Our Perspective 11

    Under Pressure 12

    Our Foundation of Greatness 13

        The Building of Our Foundation 15

        Leaders Help Us Become Our Best Selves 16

The Journey to Unleashing Greatness. 17

Transformation Is Possible. 19

Questions to Consider 19

Chapter Takeaways 19

**CHAPTER 1 - STORIES THAT REVEAL OUR
FOUNDATION** **21**

Stories on My Journey. 22

Serving Others *22*

Setting High Expectations *23*

Learning and Growing *24*

Untapped Intrinsic Energy. *24*

Why? For What Purpose?. *25*

Flow—It Feels Right *27*

A Recipe for Sustainable Success *28*

Our Personal Fit *29*

Have a Vision *30*

The Role of Foundational Stories 32

Questions to Consider 32

Chapter Takeaways 33

**CHAPTER 2 - YOUR CORE IDENTITY: THE ENABLER
OF SUSTAINABLE GREATNESS.** **35**

The Key Enablers of Sustainable Success. 35

Your Core Identity *35*

Reinforcing Systems *36*

Your Core Identity Enables Flow 36

Five Stages of Organizational Flow *37*

The First Two Core Identity Components: A Compelling
Purpose and Vision 38

Energized by Our Purpose and Vision *39*

Our Motivation: Our Four Stages of Fulfillment 41

*Living a Fulfilled, Meaningful Life, True to Our Purpose
and Vision* *41*

Making the Connection to Our Life's Purpose *42*

Stage I Fulfillment: Meeting Our Primary Physical Needs *43*

Stage II Fulfillment: Learning, Growing, and Competing *45*

Stage III Fulfillment: Benefiting Others *47*

Stage IV Fulfillment: Creating a Better Tomorrow *51*

Story of the Stages of Fulfillment *52*

Everything We Do Should Be in Service of Our Vision. *52*

How Visions Become Reality—The Reticular Activating System . . *54*

The Third Core Identity Component: Guiding Principles
for Working at Our Best Together 56

Guiding Principles—What They Do. *57*

The Role of Feelings and Our Guiding Principles 58

Leadership's Sensitivity to Feelings *59*

Two Essential Guiding Principles: Trust and Caring 60

Trust *61*

Caring. *62*

Build Trust and Caring with Actions. *62*

Clarifying the Boundaries of Our Guiding Principles 64

Questions to Consider 66

Chapter Takeaways 66

**CHAPTER 3 - CULTURE CLARIFICATION: REVEALING
THE GREATNESS THAT RESIDES IN YOUR
ORGANIZATION** **67**

Preparing the Team 68

Surveys and Interviews *68*

The Team Engagement Process *70*

Preparing Leadership 70

Attributes of Exceptional Leaders *71*

Leadership and Listening *82*

Revealing Your Core Identity 84

The Retreat: Expectations *84*

The Key Role of Storytelling *86*

Revealing the Organization's Guiding Principles *87*

Allowing Feelings to Be Expressed *88*

Revealing the Organization's Shared Purpose *89*

Revealing the Organization's Compelling Shared Vision *90*

Individual Identities Meld into a Shared Core Identity *91*

Honoring Your Core Identity 91

Essential Success Factors *91*

Critical Failure Factors *93*

Choosing Success or Failure *93*

A New "At Our Best" 94

The Retreat Experience *94*

Questions to Consider 96

Chapter Takeaways 96

CHAPTER 4 – REINFORCING SUSTAINABLE SUCCESS . . 99

Reinforcing Systems Support Peak Performance 101

    The Effectiveness of Disciplined Reinforcing Systems. *103*

    Clarify the Boundaries. *103*

    Capitalizing on Your Foundation of Greatness. *106*

    Aligning Habits for the Team *107*

    Leaders Need to Listen to Dissenters *110*

    Fit—Alignment with the Core Identity *111*

Committees Can Institutionalize Your Culture 113

    Committees Set Bottom-up Disciplines *116*

The Enablers of Peak Performance 117

    The Peak Performance Equation *118*

    The Peak Performance Evaluation *120*

Closing the Performance Gap 121

Assessing the Performance Gap 122

    Assess Operating Systems First. *123*

    Assessing Team Members *124*

    Metrics for Individual, Department, and Organizational
    Responsibility *126*

Leadership's Role in Encouraging Bottom-up Alignment. . . . 129

    Support of Core Identity Committees *130*

    Shared Responsibility for Decision-Making *131*

Exemplary Leaders Give Control *132*

Clarifying Boundaries of the Core Identity *132*

Addressing Out-of-Bounds Behavior *136*

Outcomes of the Shift from *Me* to *Team* 138

We Think like a Team *138*

We are Envisioning Future Success *138*

We Create Safety and Security *139*

We Are on a Trusted Journey Together *140*

Our Core Identity Is Our Compass for Dynamic Strategic Planning . *141*

Questions to Consider 141

Chapter Takeaways 141

CHAPTER 5: DYNAMIC STRATEGIC PLANNING 143

Preparing for Tomorrow 143

Start with Your Vision: Where Do You Want to Go? *145*

Be Dynamically Responsive *146*

Commit to a Disciplined Process *146*

The Process of Dynamic Strategic Planning 148

Where Are We on the Journey? *148*

What Are Your Vision Objectives? *149*

Create Initiatives to Close the Vision Gaps *150*

Systematizing Dynamic Strategic Planning *151*

Examples of Dynamic Strategic Planning and the Results *154*

Greatness Unleashed, Greatness Sustained 156

Questions to Consider 157

Chapter Takeaways 157

CHAPTER 6: LEADERSHIP OF THE FUTURE **159**

The Team Member of the Future: Expectations 162

Serving a Higher Purpose *162*

Sustainability. *165*

Diverse Perspectives *165*

Flexible Work Hours, Four-Day Workweek *166*

Side Hustles *166*

The Subtle Shift for Leaders 167

Understanding the Desire to Be Cared About *168*

The Perception of Respect and Being Cared About. *168*

80% Is Not Good Enough *169*

People Are Doing the Best They Can *170*

Leaders Build Relationships *171*

Be Curious; Be Open to Learning and Growing *172*

The Core Purpose of Leadership: Close the Peak Performance Gap. . *173*

Questions to Consider. .174

Chapter Takeaways 175

CLOSING. **177**

APPENDIXES **179**

Appendix A: Extraordinary Teams Survey: Beyond
High Performance 179

Appendix B: Peak Performance Assessment Template 180

Appendix C: Resources for the Reader 183

ABOUT THE AUTHOR. **185**

INDEX **187**

FOREWORD

Serendipity has always been an important factor in my life, as illustrated in this example. The year was 2015, and I had just taken my first department chair position. The department I was brought in to lead had fallen on hard times. Most faculty had left the department, the residency training program was on probation, and morale was very low. A few months after I started, I attended the 2016 Association of University Professors of Ophthalmology annual meeting, where I signed up for a "breakfast with the experts" on the topic of difficult conversations. I was certainly having quite a few such conversations in the early months of my chairmanship, and I thought I would benefit from the wisdom of the experienced colleague leading the discussion. It was at this roundtable that I first heard about Fritz Seyferth and his work. It is truly not an overstatement to say that this breakfast changed my life, both professionally and personally. I often think how different my leadership path might have been had I not attended this breakfast!

When I returned home from the meeting, I emailed Fritz to find out how the process of culture clarification could help my department. We had many discussions over the ensuing months, and I was finally able to convince the leadership at my institution that hiring Fritz and his team was a valuable investment in the future of the department, although some did remain skeptical. Over the next three years, Fritz and his team worked with everyone in the department. There was a great deal of hard work and many difficult conversations along the way, but the result was spectacular. By 2019, we were the top department in the institution in terms of both physician and employee engagement, our residency was thriving, and there was a palpable feeling of collegiality and community among the entire team. It put us in a good position to weather the unexpected events of 2020.

My personal leadership journey has been greatly enriched by what I have learned in my work with Fritz. Physicians, especially surgeons, are not used to thinking about the types of things that are detailed in this book, but they are essential to being the best leader one can be. I know that you will learn from the many insights within this volume if you are open to looking at yourself and others with fresh eyes. Enjoy!

Kathryn Colby, MD, PhD
New York, NY
June 2022

PREFACE

Happiness cannot be pursued; it must ensue.

—Viktor E. Frankl,
Man's Search for Meaning

I have been blessed to spend more than fifty years observing leaders in athletics and business. Athletics is a public laboratory for all to witness both effective and disastrous leadership. It is easy for us to see the players absorb and execute the coach's instructions. We see coaches with no budget and little support win championships year after year, and others with almost unlimited resources struggle. The exceptional coaches have more athletes who want to play for them than they can accommodate. The stories of these exceptional coaches are legendary. The players love them, and they enjoy being a part of the team. It is an emotional connection that feels right, and the organization receives a remarkable return on investment.

There are family-run companies and even larger organizations where leaders create the same feelings among their team members. Unfortunately, they are rarer than they need to be.

We have all witnessed and experienced stressful, de-energizing, and unhealthy cultures. Research has shown us this does not need to be. There are ways we can work better together. They include respecting human nature and our evolution as a society on how we survive and thrive together. Our work lives can be rewarding, meaningful, energizing, and good for our mental and physical health, and the leader makes all the difference.

Each of us possesses a Foundation of Greatness, and every team has a collective Foundation of Greatness. The exceptional leaders understand how to tap into each team member's greatness to surface the team's greatness for sustainable success.

Leaders who seek to be their best as coaches, teachers, mentors, and true leaders are on a constant personal growth journey to being their best selves in service of others. They are shifting from a *me*-centered focus to a *team* focus grounded in deep caring, building trust, and creating a safe place to thrive together.

I have studied exceptional leaders and their practices for many decades. In these pages, I will share findings valuable to anyone who desires to become that exceptional, transformative leader.

Our executive coaching firm, FS/A, was hired by an auto parts manufacturer to support the leadership team. At the start, it was an authoritative organization where leaders were taught to tell others what to do. The new approach we introduced made positive energy in the organization palpable. Fully engaged team members felt valued and began thriving, and their sales have quadrupled in the last ten years.

This work applies to a single person influencing interested observers, parents leading their families, politicians leading their communities, coaches leading their teams, and CEOs leading their organizations. The principles and disciplines shared connect with the core of who we are meant to be as respected, valued, and appreciated individuals.

This passion for helping build teams that thrive together has led me to a rewarding life, a life I would not have found without incredible mentors who opened my eyes to the difference I could make. I hope this book opens the door for you to thrive by positively impacting the lives of those you care about.

ACKNOWLEDGMENTS

Observing leaders who guided their teams to sustainable success inspired me to write this book. These remarkable leaders saw untapped greatness in their teams, who were committed to serving something significant and deeply meaningful.

I have had the good fortune to witness outstanding leadership. My first coaches were my amazing parents, who lived and loved life to the fullest. I had a mom who told me, "I can see you as president of the United States someday," and a father who declared, "You can fail in trying, but you will never fail to try!"

My sisters, Jane and Lisa, and my brother, Steve, supported me, even though I received disproportionate attention. Each is an exceptional person who deserves the spotlight.

My wife, Lynn, has stabilized our wonderful family journey—we have three children and twelve grandchildren, who bring joy into our lives daily. We look at our children as our life's report cards. Because of Lynn, our family life continues to yield abundant blessings.

And there have been so many others, from my Pop Warner Football coaches to the exemplary leader Bo Schembechler, legendary head coach of the Michigan Football team. I learned from him both as a player and as part of his staff. The great ones helped reveal my life's purpose: "To help others go places they never dreamt possible."

I was blessed to play football at the University of Michigan with amazing teammates who won championships together. We were challenged to play and live to a high standard. Fifty years later, we continue to hold each other to that high standard and have deep love and respect for one another.

My coaching mentor, Don McMillan, challenges me almost every day to be a better coach, with inspiration backed by more data and research than I can grasp.

Our team at FS/A of Mary Walker, Percy Bates, Jim Richardson, and Beth Ressler are energized to help people live the fulfilled life they deserve.

Given that I'm an engineer, not a writer, producing this book was a team effort, starting with my wife, Lynn, whose patience in the process has been a gift and who has read every version. Also, as a part of the FS/A team, Regan Parker organized the first draft, and Rachel Heydlauff took that to a higher level. The incredibly gifted author Patrick Flores-Scott restructured and created a flow for the book and brought it to life with client interviews. Copy editor Janet Max's diligence in refining and shaping the manuscript has been a real gift.

Jim Hume and his team at PhireGroup prepared the graphics for this book and, being a client and practicing advocate, helped clarify our message.

I hope you appreciate and cherish those who see more in you than you see in yourself. We all need someone in our lives who believe in us. I am grateful for this opportunity to share how we can be on a journey to living an energized, fulfilled, and thriving life as we shift from *me* to *team*.

THE PROBLEM WE ADDRESS

The Decline in Employee Engagement

Gallup's 2021 employee engagement survey revealed a disappointing trend. In 2020, only 36% of employees were engaged in their work, and in 2021 that number dropped to 34%. To make matters worse, the number of employees who were disengaged rose from 14% in 2020 to 16% in 2021. And this is costly—disengaged workers have higher rates of absenteeism, more accidents, and produce work with more errors and defects than their engaged counterparts.

Survey results indicate that management did not have the tools to address challenges before the COVID pandemic effectively, and leadership continues to flounder with the new challenges COVID has brought.

How can we help leaders create an environment for thriving at work?

The Team Is Struggling

Human beings are wired to accomplish, achieve, and make things better; this is how our civilization has thrived. Each of us wants to contribute to making things better and live a life that is valued. No one wants to be average!

Leaders are doing the best they can to guide and inspire their team members. But we have ignored how humans are wired to live and work together, and leaders have not experienced or been taught how to honor these fundamental principles.

From the CEO/doctor of a medical practice

"I bought a practice from a friend in his sixties. And while he's a great practitioner, he doesn't approach things like I do. He approaches it more the way most others do. More like, 'These people are here to work for us; we pay them. They should do what we ask them,' versus, 'These people want to help us be amazing by supporting one another.'"

As a result, many of our team members go home frustrated and de-energized from their day's work. This frustration impacts their work life as well as their home life. They know that something does not feel right. These feelings are genuine and very strong.

As team members are frustrated, so is leadership. Leadership is disappointed in the low level of dedication and commitment of many of their team members, and they spend too much time fixing recurring problems that surface. Leaders ask: *Why don't people do what we tell them to do? I cannot be any clearer! Don't they see how hard leadership is working?*

Leadership is doing the best they can with what they know. Leadership's challenge is that they do not know what they do not know.

This book will share timeless principles for facing today's challenges. We will expand your understanding of how these principles come together to honor how human beings are meant to work together. Our ancestors honored them to get us to where we are today. The philosophers Aristotle, Plato, and Socrates discussed the principles of human nature to illuminate how we work best together. This book shares how leaders can help their organizations achieve sustainable and natural success.

INTRODUCTION

A well-functioning organization is like a river flowing down a mountainside. There is a natural energy, and there is momentum that provides flow as we honor the natural forces of human nature.

The State of Flow

What would it feel like to have your team on the same page, fully engaged, doing their best work to benefit the organization?

Can you recall a day, a meeting, or a gathering where every moment seemed to go smoothly, the events unfolding effortlessly, almost as if they had been orchestrated? The experience feels like a river running easily and naturally, gaining momentum to its destination. The late psychologist Mihaly Csikszentmihalyi used the term *flow* to describe this psychological state of optimal performance and engagement.

When I think about the term *flow*, my mind goes back to one of University of Michigan Football's most analyzed plays against our chief rival, the Ohio State Buckeyes.

Two years before, Head Coach Bo Schembechler's first at Michigan, the football team had unexpectedly beaten the highly favored and undefeated reigning National Champion Buckeyes. That victory earned Michigan the Big Ten Conference Championship. The next year, Michigan and Ohio State were undefeated when the Buckeyes won in a close game. It was time to see if that first-year victory and championship had been a fluke or if a new era of Michigan football was beginning.

Michigan was behind by four points with two minutes to go in the game. Tension gripped the more than 100,000 fans in Michigan Stadium. Michigan quarterback Larry Cipa called a sweep from twenty-one yards outside Ohio State's goal line. We executed to perfection, with every player doing his job. As a result, we scored, capping an undefeated season, the Big Ten Championship, and a trip to the Rose Bowl.

Our running back, Billy Taylor, scored the touchdown, and to this day, he is regularly celebrated in Michigan Football highlights. I was fortunate to throw the last block, enabling Billy to score.

All eyes were focused on Billy and me. However, a detailed analysis of this play revealed that, without the contribution of each of the other nine Michigan players, Billy would not have scored.

That play was the essence of flow, but the enablers of the flow were in place long before the game. By the time the Ohio State game rolled around, we were prepared. Every player executed the high standard they were trained for by our coaches in practices, which were as intense as any game situation we would ever face.

The preparation created a sense of calm, of confidence that we had been here before. For us, the game slowed down. The pressure of the big game became a positive, energizing force, elevating our awareness. As the game unfolded, we felt like we knew what had to be done. Regardless of what the Buckeyes threw at us, our response was instinctive and natural. Even though we were behind with time running out, we knew we were going to win.

As players, we didn't fully understand the depth of what the coaching staff was doing at the time. We knew they were pushing each of us beyond what we thought possible. While they set high standards, we knew they cared deeply about us by how they treated us off the field. It was about each of us individually being the best we could be for the team. Working for each other energized us, but there was a more profound responsibility we were taught. In everything we did, Bo and his coaches connected us to our responsibility to honor the Michigan tradition, the people who came before, and the high standards expected of Michigan.

The feeling of flow resulted from our working together to get better and better. We were motivated by a culture built on an ideal more significant than any individual. Our responsibility was bigger than us—it was about honoring the ideal of Michigan to sustain something that would last far beyond our time. It was about doing it together as good stewards for future generations. It was a team where no one person was more important than another. This ideal set the stage for the natural flow of our execution.

The Enablers of Sustainable Greatness

After playing professional football, a fast-track corporate career as an engineer and consultant left me feeling unfulfilled. I found myself back at Michigan Football, responsible for all off-the-field operations. At Michigan, I was driven to understand if there was a strategy or science behind truly exceptional teams. Could this success be systematized? Over the next fourteen years, I studied the most extraordinary leaders of the most outstanding teams to differentiate what they were doing to achieve consistent success. This study revealed a foundation for decision-making that was clear to all and honored how they achieved Peak Performance. We call this honoring the Foundation of Greatness.

Several years after leaving Michigan Athletics, I founded FS/A. For more than twenty years, our FS/A team has been helping organizations uncover their Foundation of Greatness to achieve consistent Peak Performance.

In the following pages, we'll describe the enablers that have helped our clients achieve that flow state for long-term sustainable success.

The Leadership Shift from *Me* to *Team*

On the journey to unleashing greatness, we ask you to challenge many commonly held beliefs about what attributes great leaders possess. Many misguided beliefs have deep roots in history.

The impact of thousands of officers coming home from WWII to lead corporate America influenced how leadership was viewed and conducted. Leadership on the front was about control, displays of authority, and expertise over young, immature soldiers. That leadership methodology was brought home by the military officers and the 18–25-year-old soldiers mentored in this fashion. This top-down authoritarian leadership style remains common today because it is easier to give orders than take the time to ask questions. Authoritarian leaders do not address unleashing the energy, passion, and creativity required for innovative productivity. Top-down leadership creates de-energizing stress, resulting in a lack of engagement in team members. This kind of stress shortens lives. *Me* leadership—*control* leadership—focuses on the leader at the team's expense.

Team-focused leadership taps into the root of how humans are meant to work together. Humans are wired to be emotionally moved and energized by the fulfillment of team success more than individual success. After all, we are the product of our ancestors, who thrived because they developed communities of interdependent people who supported each other and had each other's backs. *Team* leadership capitalizes on the human desire to succeed as a team and be part of a community.

The enabling of individual greatness requires the leader to be genuinely curious about how they may best serve the organization and its culture. They must ask many questions and take in the answers, allowing decision-making to flow from the bottom up. This process will not be as immediately efficient as telling others how to execute the plan. However, *team-focused* leadership creates the foundation for producing extraordinary results. This is only possible when a leader acknowledges that the collective intelligence, talents, and gifts are more significant than their own. Leaders who move to *team-focused* leadership enable sustainable greatness, and they experience a deep sense of fulfillment in their work. The enablers of sustainable greatness can surface once the leader—and each team member—embrace their roles as *one team with a shared vision*. We refer to this as the *Shift from Me to Team*.

> *From the CEO of a marketing/branding agency*
>
> *"This process allowed me to let go and let my team define what the company was all about. I used to think that was my job. I bit my lip a lot during this process. It hurt a lot. But I realized this was the only way we will become sustainable. Otherwise, it's just me dictating, me telling people.*
>
> *"At our Culture Clarification retreat, I mostly sat in the corner and observed. I participated when it was necessary but didn't overrule or override anything. I just let it happen. It was insightful and eye-opening when I heard other people talk about the company. And largely, it was successfully unearthing the things I would have said and done. So, it was there. It was there in the company. The team needed to define it and live it. So that was the first step in opening my eyes."*

Most leaders climb the ladder by capitalizing upon their talent and skill to deliver results. Leaders are now tasked with *leading others* who deliver the results. This requires a shift from what the leader thinks to what their team needs. This shift enables leaders to create a thriving culture that unleashes their team's greatness.

The shift from Me leadership to Team leadership means leaders no longer demand that their team serve them. It is bigger than them. Their responsibility is to energize their team members to serve their shared Purpose.

For Peak Performance, the shift from *me* to *team* needs to reside in every individual in the organization. But it begins with the leader. The shift from *me* leadership to *team* leadership is challenging, and it takes time. Accepting the challenge head-on is what this book is about, and the rewards go beyond expectations.

Our Perspective

Each of us is born with a unique set of gifts and talents. We learn from our good and bad decisions as we blaze our trail through the jungle of life. We begin to develop feelings for what is right and wrong. This is a big part of who we are becoming as we journey on our unique path. Our challenge is that the path we have been on is a mere sliver of life's opportunities for experiences. Yet once we are far enough down the path, we feel we have answers; we have things figured out. The reality is we do not have answers—we only have our perspective.

The best solution is found in valuing the meshing and merging of the collective perspectives of team members. Each of us possesses our unique perspective, and together, with trust and respect, we can create the best answer possible. And we still can be wrong! However, we have achieved our responsibility to be the best we can be, and if wrong, we learn together for better decision-making in the future.

We like to use the imagery of the moon, which has a light side and a dark side. How many of us have gotten into an argument because we don't see the other side of the moon?

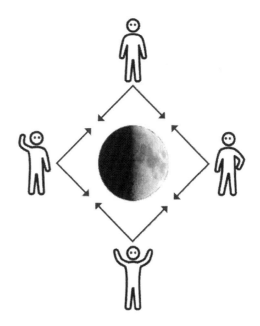

Contributing Our Perspective, Not the Answer

A surgeon/client on perspective

"We are surgeons, and we are used to making decisions by ourselves and getting the credit for our success. The FS/A culture process has taught us to think of others more and think in our team's best interest for the benefit of our patients.

"I was surprised at the impact of giving power to the team. Instead of saying, 'Here's the solution,' we let the team develop a solution. It's like a magical thing. It works much better than my telling them, even if it is the same solution, and sometimes it's better than mine.

"Because we created our Guiding Principles together, we call each other on perceived boundary violations. These principles belong to our department, not any one of us. We try to have a non-hierarchical team as much as possible. We strive to create a team where all have the power to say something, to contribute.

"It's hard. We try to create this feeling that everyone is equal in contributing to the team. Even though the contribution varies, everyone plays a role in our success. There's still a hierarchy, but it works. People work well together for the good of everybody."

Under Pressure

Like looking at the moon and only see what is visible from Earth, we may only see half of the problem on a good day, which is the reality in most conflicts or challenges. Unfortunately, when we are under pressure, we see even less due to the stress on our physiology. We may see only one-quarter of an issue, but we dig in to protect our self-esteem because we feel threatened in this state. This often results in embarrassment and our losing trust by not being open to another's perspective.

To be effective, the leader needs to understand that when under pressure, seeking more diverse perspectives is important. The leader needs to shift into thinking what is best for the team, not themselves. The team members will respect that they are valued, and they will more fully contribute to the organization's success; ultimately the leader will receive the credit for the team's success.

Our Foundation of Greatness

The shift from *me* to *team* begins with the leader's responsibility to unleash the dormant greatness that resides naturally in each team member. Concurrently, the leader unleashes their personal best self as they shift from *me* to *team*. This opens the door to tap into human nature's desire for sustainable greatness.

In her book *Conversational Intelligence,* Judith Glaser shares that all mammals possess a primitive brain that is emotionally reactive and fear-avoidant. It is there to protect us and is where we go when stressed. We fight, flee, or freeze when we are fearful or in an unfamiliar place. We resist change, are skeptical, and go inside for decision-making. When threatened, we are secreting the stress hormone cortisol, which prepares us to fight tigers but is not good for us to live with for long periods. For example, the first few public speaking experiences can be frightening, and they may generate a stress response.

Fortunately, we are blessed with an executive brain that thinks about the longer term. It uses wisdom, creativity, strategy, and empathy to gain foresight, insight, and trust. It starts with trusting that together we can be better tomorrow. It is about co-creation and partnering together for a better outcome. In this state, we are secreting oxytocin, a feel-good hormone that is good for us. Repeated experiences of speaking publicly permit the executive brain to teach the primitive brain that there is much less to fear than first felt.

As we seek to help others, our best self surfaces. As we learn to be more vulnerable, we become more of the person and the leader we are meant to be. It is natural for us to gain new confidence in ourselves by partnering with and being open to what others see. We become much more effective as a leader and a doer, and life begins to flow more effortlessly.

It's often difficult to see the best in others. When FS/A comes on board to work with an organization, we can see things from the leader's perspective. In difficult cases, team members are stressed, and some may have developed bad habits. There may be a culture of mistrust, a feeling of powerlessness, and a lack of meaning in their work.

If any of this sounds familiar, it makes sense that you might view some team members as uninspired, dysfunctional, or combative.

We have learned from experience that most of those individuals are working at their best. But they are in an environment that has not permitted their natural greatness to be tapped.

We worked with the chair of a major academic medical department who, upon their hiring, was told, "You can fire every one of your faculty. There needs to be a change in this department." This was not true in this case, and we have never found this to be accurate; we are doubtful it could ever be true. In our work, we have found that among the employees at all levels of the organization:

- Approximately 20% are "A" players who role model what is best for the organization.
- Approximately 20% will be a challenge to the culture of their organization.
- Approximately 60% need support and guidance; they can follow either of the above groups.

While we have found that not all people are the right fit, we have never found it necessary to replace everyone.

The Building of Our Foundation

We believe that each of us possesses a foundation for us to be sustainably successful. This is our Foundation of Greatness. It begins with the unique set of gifts each of us is born with. As we journey through the jungle of life, we encounter forks in the road. As we make decisions, some good and some bad, we learn and gain a feeling for the right thing to do to be successful. As we make good and bad decisions, we learn and grow, building our foundation for decision-making.

At FS/A, we have yet to work with a leader who hasn't demonstrated their insecurities. To some degree, everyone is insecure. With a deeper understanding of our Foundation of Greatness, we gain greater confidence and can go into very stressful and difficult situations knowing we will come out just fine. We know who we are, and we respect who we are trying to become.

This Foundation of Greatness is composed of these elements:

- disciplined responsibility to honor the organization's Peak Performance Core Identity
  - Purpose
  - Vision
  - Guiding Principles
- competencies for the work to be done at the highest level for the job
  - talents
  - skills
  - knowledge

- appropriate behavior under pressure for each job
  - positivity
  - passion for the work
  - appropriate behavior for the job

Leaders Help Us Become Our Best Selves

As we journey through the jungle of life, we build a foundation for decision-making based on our unique set of talents, knowledge, and experiences. We are energized by some people and events and de-energized by others. This journey informs how we make decisions and who we desire to be. In addition, we begin to understand our gifts and what it feels like to live our best life. When we live and work honoring who we are meant to be, it feels right to us. When we honor who we are meant to be, we feel energized, motivated, and alive. We see and feel the possibility of becoming more. Our life is on a journey, congruent with where we feel we should be headed.

That said, each of us is on a journey to build that foundation for better decision-making. Each of us is doing our best with our unique set of assets and deficiencies and with the limitations of our perspective. And even when we are under extraordinary stress or feel depleted, we are doing the best we can.

Great leaders understand this, and if underperformance by a team member is an issue, then leadership must look at their responsibilities:

- hiring the right person
- training and coaching
- providing the required assets
- inspiring continued growth

When a team member succeeds, it is the team member's doing. When a team member fails, it is the leader's deficit in one of the above requirements for success.

Enabling team members to thrive is the recipe for sustainable success. There is a Foundation of Greatness resident in each individual on your team. This foundation is deep; it is a collective well of untapped energy with significant potential. As a leader, achieving greatness is about tapping into that collective well by creating a culture where everyone feels safe and secure, where everyone's contributions are valued and recognized. The right team members are energized by the belief that, at its core, the organization is striving to positively impact people's lives.

The Journey to Unleashing Greatness

At FS/A, we have an audacious goal: for the hours spent at work to be among the best hours of the day. As a bonus, team members often take home what they learn. We hear stories of transformation within their families, as well as the positive impact on boards of directors they serve on. Their lives are richer as they learn to shift from a *me* focus to a *team* focus. They realize this is how we are meant to work and live together.

In the chapters that follow, we will describe the process we have developed to help our clients reach sustainable Peak Performance.

Chapter 1 – Stories That Reveal Our Foundation – I challenge you to reflect upon your unique life journey. Just as individuals have stories that have shaped who they have become, each organization possesses stories of performing at its best. I will share personal experiences that have shaped or revealed who I have become so far. You and your organization have similar illuminating stories.

Chapter 2 – Your Core Identity: The Enabler of Sustainable Greatness – There is a foundation that enables long-term, sustainable success. This is the foundation for all decision-making. The foundation is built on the components of your Core Identity:

- a deep and meaningful shared **_Purpose_** that aligns with each team member
- a shared **_Vision_** that inspires all to work today at their best to have a transformative, meaningful impact
- a shared set of **_Guiding Principles_** that define how the team works best together in service of their Purpose and Vision

Chapter 3 – Culture Clarification: Revealing the Greatness That Resides in Your Organization – We share the processes FS/A uses to help teams reveal and clarify their Core Identity.

Chapter 4 – Reinforcing Sustainable Success – How can we ensure that the Core Identity permeates every aspect of the organization? Reinforcing Systems create better habits that remind and support team members in honoring the organization at its best.

Chapter 5 – Dynamic Strategic Planning – This is the real purpose of our daily work: to become purposefully better tomorrow than we are today for long-term safety and security. Your organization's Vision guides Dynamic Strategic Planning to create a better tomorrow. We share how you can instill the disciplines required for dynamic and purposeful movement toward that Vision.

Chapter 6 – Leadership of the Future – This chapter outlines the essential attributes for tomorrow's leaders and addresses these questions: How will leaders lead so organizations thrive? What role can organizations play in creating better lives?

Transformation Is Possible

Throughout decades of doing this work, we have witnessed transformation—from de-energized and stressed to energized and fulfilled—as leaders engage with team members and value their contributions to organizational decision-making.

We will share stories and testimonials throughout the book that exemplify this transformation.

As you read, I challenge you to hold onto the idea that a Foundation of Greatness is resident in you and every one of *your team members*. Imagine what might be possible if you tapped into each team member's greatness in service of the team. Picture your workplace humming with the feeling of *energized flow*, and imagine a culture that leads to thriving and having a sustainable impact on the lives of others.

Questions to Consider

- Are you reflective? Do you regularly assess the effectiveness of your actions, imagining what a better outcome would look like next time?
- Are you taking the time to tap into the greatness resident in each team member?
- Are you curious? Do you seek to understand better your team members' perspectives and why they think the way they do?
- Can you delay short-term gratification as you seek long-term safety and security for those in your organization?

Chapter Takeaways

- There are enablers of flow each of us seek at home and work.

- A study of the enablers reveals components of how we can have positive and predictable results in the future.
- The move from a *me* mindset to a *team* mindset is at the core of leadership transformation.
- Humans are wired to care for and protect each other for the long term.
- There is natural greatness in each of us seeking to be unleashed.
- Great leaders tap into the individual greatness of each team member for sustainable success.

CHAPTER 1

STORIES THAT REVEAL
OUR FOUNDATION

If you want to change the world, you need to change your story. This truth applies both to individuals and institutions.

—MICHAEL MARGOLIS

Each of us is on a unique journey through the jungle of life. As we face and overcome challenges, as we interact with and observe others, our experiences leave us with feelings; some are good, and others are not so good. Our unique identity is developed through our sense of what feels right and what feels wrong. For each of us, it is the feelings in these foundational stories that shape or reveal who we are.

Our challenge is to take time to contemplate the meaning of these foundational stories, thereby better understanding who we are. As we gain a deeper appreciation of our struggles, triumphs, and gifts, we see that our stories reveal the person we are today and shed light on our journey to becoming the person we are meant to be.

An organization's journey is the synthesis of the team members' journeys. It is not the logo, the building, or even the product. Storytelling reveals the natural greatness of organizations that choose to embark on the *me* to *team* journey. The organization's greatness gets better understood, reinforced, and honored through storytelling.

As Steve Jobs said, *"You can't connect the dots looking forward; you can only connect them looking back. So, you have to trust that the dots will somehow connect in your future."*

Stories on My Journey

Stories are powerful. Our life-impacting stories reveal a great deal about who we are and who we are meant to become. To aid in your self-discovery, I'd like to share a few stories that have shaped me and helped reveal who I am thus far on my journey. This is an exercise we do with clients, and these are the stories that surfaced when I did this for myself the first time. These stories surface the values, gifts, and learnings that are most important to me. They are stepping stones for my journey to becoming my best self.

Serving Others

When I was young, my father's job with Scott Paper Company meant we moved a lot. As a salesman, he was on the road during the week, but it was all about family on weekends. We were either at the ball fields together or working around the house and the yard together. *The family was to be valued.*

My dad had high expectations for himself. He had an inspirational work ethic, and he cared about every detail. Whether it was a work presentation, mowing our yard, or volunteering with the recreational leagues in Covina, California; Swarthmore, Pennsylvania; or Darien, Connecticut, he took on tasks big and small, and each outcome was a masterpiece. *We learned if you are going to do something, do it well.*

When my brother, Steve, sisters Jane and Lisa, and I came of age, we all played team sports, with Dad coaching our teams. It was important to him that we and all the other children in our neighborhood played on well-prepared fields and received high-quality coaching, and he provided both. *Caring about providing the resources for others to succeed is important.*

Dad's teams always competed for the league championship. He was tough on us because he saw more in us than we saw in ourselves. He had a way of getting us to play at a higher level than we had ever experienced. *He wanted us to realize who we could become.*

My dad led with the Guiding Principles of *integrity* and *caring*, and his commitment was especially apparent in the championship game at the end of one season. According to his rules, you played in the next game if you made all the practices and prepared with a positive attitude. We were behind by one run in the last inning. The bases were loaded with two outs. Keeping his commitment, Dad put in the last player who had not been in the game yet. To the player's credit, he took the pitcher to a full count—three balls and two strikes—before striking out and ending the game; we lost the championship. We were all disappointed, but we all knew we played the game the way it was meant to be played, with integrity and caring. We eventually got over the hurt of losing, but *the importance of integrity and caring stayed.*

Dad's messages have stuck: *Success is a process.*

Setting High Expectations

As a kid, I struggled to read and write. I most likely was dyslexic, but that was unknown to us at the time. My mom understood my struggle, yet she never changed her expectations for who I could become, often saying, "You will be the president one day." Mom required that I come home from school and finish my homework before going out to play with my friends. When I struggled to write a paper, she would ask me what I wanted it to say. Sitting at our white Formica kitchen counter, she would write out my thoughts on the counter in pencil, and I would then rewrite them for my paper. Like my dad with baseball, my mom was always there to help with my schooling. But more importantly, she taught me that obstacles are merely challenges to overcome. *Obstacles are just challenges to overcome.*

Learning and Growing

My mother was a creative free spirit. She believed rules were not meant to be taken at face value. *We were to think.* We'd better understand why specific rules are made and whether they are getting the intended results. In analyzing the rules, we'd come to respect them, or we'd learn that some rules were counterproductive.

To this day, my siblings and I are still curious about rules! We share a strong desire to understand how things work and how they might work better. We analyze ideas, trying to make sense of them. I know this relates to my mom's way of seeing the world: We do not accept what we see at face value. We question it. We try to understand. We assess and decide. Then we examine our decision—could it be better? *Be analytical and be reflective.*

Untapped Intrinsic Energy

I have always been fascinated by why things work the way they do. As a kid, I would take apart bicycles and just about anything else I could disassemble. Then I would put it back together to better understand why it worked or perhaps how I could make it better.

This fascination led me to a degree in Industrial and Operations Engineering at the University of Michigan. I would also play football as a walk-on on Bump Elliott's last Wolverine team and then three years on Bo Schembechler's first teams. At the time, collegiate head football coaches were the most impressive leaders I had ever met. The combination of their passion for caring for you, their high standards for everyone around them, and the way they seemingly always knew the right thing to do and say under pressure was inspiring. These men started me on my study of exceptional leaders who made everyone around them better.

After a short stint playing football for the New York Giants and Calgary Stampeders that provided more leadership stories, I took on my first engineering consulting job with BF Goodrich in Akron, Ohio; I traveled North America fixing plant problems. I left that job after realizing I was challenged with improving plant operations—through tens of millions of dollars of expenditures—yet none of the changes or the dollars addressed the real problems.

One night at 3:00 a.m., I observed the third-shift plant operations. I found the "maxed to capacity" equipment idle. I went to the union steward and asked why the plant was not running. He said, "Today is Thursday. Come back tomorrow and see what we do." I had no idea what that meant, but I did know that the central issue was not more machines, better layouts, or better materials—it was people. Our leadership thought success was determined by investment in equipment and processes. The reality is that an investment in the energy level and motivation of the workforce will help meet production demands better than equipment.

People have intrinsic energy in them, ready and available to be tapped. Human potential may be the most underutilized asset organizations possess.

Why? For What Purpose?

Encountering this lack of understanding that success is about people led me to seek another job. My wife, Lynn, son, Sean, and I moved to Connecticut, where I went to work for Arthur Young & Co. By taking this job, I had accomplished the dream of working in a prestigious corporate consulting firm in New York City. Our office handled Fortune 50 companies. Daily, I rubbed elbows with people who had a tangible and significant impact on the business world.

Soon, I had a wife and two young children at home in Connecticut and an apartment in Providence, Rhode Island, for client work, all while getting my MBA at night school. I enjoyed working with clients, and I enjoyed coming home on weekends, but something was missing. Life did not feel right. Lynn felt it, too, sharing, "Something is going to change!"

Soon after this realization, I had dinner with my managing partner. I was in my late twenties. He was in his mid-forties and was sharp and well-educated. He had worked hard to get to where he was. He drove a beautiful car and had homes in Florida, Connecticut, and Vermont. He seemed to have everything I was working to achieve.

As we waited for our food to arrive, I noticed tears streaming down his face. I asked him what was wrong. He said, "Today's my son's sixteenth birthday, and I don't even know him."

I realized I was looking into my future. I connected with his feelings and found the same surfacing in me. *Is this what I want for my life?*

That Friday, I returned home and saw my New York Giants' 8x10 headshot taped to the refrigerator. I asked Lynn about it, and she said she put it there so our children wouldn't forget what their father looked like.

Six months later, life hit us with a sledgehammer. I was commuting two hours each way consulting with Knickerbocker Toy Company in New Jersey. I got a call from a next-door neighbor, and she was crying as she told me I had to come home. Our two-year-old son Sean was comatose with complications from the flu, and an ambulance had taken him to the hospital.

I spent five days with Sean in the hospital. I decided to make a change. From that day forward, I would prioritize my family, and I was going to be there for my wife and kids.

The word got out, and I received a call from University of Michigan Football coach Bo Schembechler. He said college football was turning into a business. "You need to run the business so I can have a whistle around my neck!" We moved to Michigan, and I joined Michigan Football as Recruiting Coordinator/Director of Football Operations.

Flow—It Feels Right

My understanding of leadership from my post-college experiences received a wake-up call on my first day with Michigan Football. It was an eye-opener!

Every day started with the entire football staff of twelve around a boardroom table. On my first day, Head Coach Bo Schembechler left the room to take a call. Five minutes later, he returned from his office and slammed the door, nearly knocking it off its hinges. He had everyone's attention.

In a clear voice, he demanded, "Which one of you promised this high school quarterback he would start as a freshman when he visited us this weekend?"

I had just arrived from Arthur Young & Co., where you kept your head down when the shrapnel started flying. The worst thing you could do was stand up and admit a mistake—doing so could end your career.

Bo's meeting room was different. Instead of hiding, two coaches stood up: Don Nehlen, who went on to be West Virginia's most celebrated head coach, and Tirrel Burton, Michigan's legendary backfield coach. They both said they had shown the recruit the current Michigan quarterbacks on film, and then they asked him if he thought he could compete as a freshman. They assured Bo they hadn't promised a thing.

I was shocked at how firmly and quickly each responded to Bo.

Bo addressed the room, capturing this reinforcing opportunity to say, "Men, there is only one way you start at Michigan. You earn it! Nothing is given; you compete for everything in this program."

Bo's reinforced message was understood. And the message went well beyond recruiting.

I hadn't witnessed anything like this transparent sharing of who we are and how we are to conduct ourselves in professional football or at BF Goodrich or Arthur Young. I had never seen a leader associate how an organization made decisions with such clarity. It felt like the natural decision-making flow we are meant to feel in life. It was clear, it was simple, and it made sense.

A Recipe for Sustainable Success

That first day as staff member at Michigan Football began my more than forty-year journey to a deeper understanding of leadership's role in achieving sustainable greatness. The enablers for sustainable success became apparent.

After nine years on the football staff, a promotion to Associate Athletic Director allowed me to implement these enablers for sustainable team success. Through this work, it became clear to me that it is human nature to act and react in ways geared towards the survival and growth of the *community*, and this is how civilization survived in the wilderness. If this is human science-based, then there must be a way to predict and systemize what motivates people to work together.

I worked with my coaches to implement the enablers, developing a system I came to call the *Foundation of Greatness*. Many of those coaches had their most successful seasons ever. In 1995, I was preparing a publication of my findings when Jim Collins and Jerry Porras published

Built to Last, their book based on six years of research on the most sustainably successful businesses. I was shocked that their study in a corporate setting validated the critical components of the Foundation of Greatness I was using for athletics. I then realized this is not about athletic teams specifically but human nature and communities in general. And we have learned even more since 1995 about how best to create sustainability.

Our Personal Fit

After being passed over twice for a promotion to Director of Athletics at Michigan, I used the Foundation of Greatness principles to help me in making my tough decision to leave the university that meant so much to me and had been an integral part of my identity. At FS/A, we share that an organization is like a garden, and team members are like plants. A king palm tree that thrives in Miami can be kept alive in Chicago, but it will be expensive, and the tree will never thrive. Like a plant that needs to find another garden, I was not a fit for what the Michigan presidents were seeking. To thrive, I had to leave Michigan Athletics.

I spent two years with a venture startup in the automotive industry. We turned an idea on a piece of paper into a company with $22 million in sales and forty-five employees. I loved building the business, but operating in an industry that lacked trust left me unfulfilled. I was in the wrong garden once again at the age of fifty-one, but I now had many more stories helping me understand who I was meant to become.

While at Michigan Athletics, I had spoken nationally about the Foundation of Greatness system for sustainable success that was integral to our outstanding teams. The response was overwhelmingly positive. I had always worked for someone else, but as I reflected on the receptivity across the country to the message, I realized it was time to leave the startup to fulfill my purpose: to help organizations on their path to sustainable greatness. Thus began FS/A.

The journey as an executive coach and team builder has been a blessing. Every day I am rewarded with growing experiences that enhance my thriving, while I help others to do the same. I feel fortunate to be on this journey guided by remarkable mentors, alongside my team and our clients. We learn from each other daily. I am thrilled that this book allows you and many others to join our journey.

A CEO reflects on the Culture Clarification process

"Now that we know how we look at our best, success is not as difficult as we were making it. We clarified why we do what we do, and how we work best together. Now we all own it. We make better decisions for the organization, and we make ourselves faster. There is less confusion, especially for me as the leader. I wondered if I was doing the right thing, and I did not like it when others questioned me. We are all in this together, though the final responsibility still resides with me. I feel better, knowing we are in this together, and if we make a mistake, we will all learn together.

"Perhaps the most significant benefit has come to us in our hiring. We have a new dimension we assess in hiring we never objectively looked at in the past. And this process has made all the difference. Our new hires are some of our best team members.

"And then it became a matter of how we make this a part of who we are as we bring on new people. How do we create a set of values that are being honored? Now that we have values and know where we're going, we can now create systems. And those systems reinforce the best path for us."

Have a Vision

How can you create a vision that impacts your life? Here is an example from my own life: I needed to cut back on the amount of food I had become used to eating as a football player. I challenged others to envision their desired future for their business and life, so I challenged myself to do the same.

To create a motivating vision for my health, I wanted to embrace these elements:

- my love for family
- my joy in taking others on their growth journey
- my appreciation for the outdoors
- my passion for downhill skiing
- the pleasure of being physically active
- the energy that comes from having fun with others

I crafted a vision statement: *To possess a fit mind, body, and spirit such that I am energized and able to teach our grandchildren and great-grandchildren how to ski.*

This is an emotionally motivating vision for me. Current ski trips with grandchildren only reinforce my desire to be here for my great-grandchildren. As a result, I am more motivated to eat, sleep, and exercise to make that possible.

Can you think of a vision that is so profoundly motivating to you that it may help you on your journey to living the life you deeply desire?

The Role of Foundational Stories

Each of us has stories that reveal who we have become as we journey through the jungle of life. These stories reveal our natural strengths, why we do what we do, and how we do it. At first, the components of who we are meant to be may be unclear, though we can feel when our principles have been honored or violated. And then, we have stories of those we do not admire. Our life-defining stories exemplify moments when we were fully energized because the purpose behind what we were doing was so powerful and meaningful.

For your organization, there is power in sharing the energizing stories from your team that reveal your organization's purpose and principles. These are the critical components of your Foundation of Greatness that guide you on your unique and natural journey to sustainable success.

For you personally, consider journaling to connect with stories that impact your life, reveal your gifts, and allow you to reflect on the person you are becoming. The power behind writing down the three energizing experiences of the day goes beyond our ability to understand what it does for us. It just works.

Questions to Consider

- What life-defining stories have brought energy into your life, and what stories have been de-energizing?
- What life-defining stories have helped reveal or have helped shape who you have become today?
- How can you capitalize upon these stories to honor and lead the thriving and fulfilling life you deserve?

Chapter Takeaways

- Who we are is in the stories we tell about ourselves and that others tell about us.

- We must connect the dots looking back to connect them moving forward effectively.

- Your feelings of right and wrong come from your experiences in life. Study those essential experiences and the feelings they evoke.

- Pay attention to your feelings and identify what values are being honored or violated.

- Creating sustainable success starts with two building blocks:
  - disciplined systems that enable the natural flow of our work
  - a compelling and clear vision of the meaningful difference you hope to make in the world

CHAPTER 2

YOUR CORE IDENTITY: THE ENABLER OF SUSTAINABLE GREATNESS

This chapter will share the components of your Core Identity that, when honored, enable your organization to enjoy successful, sustainable flow—the feeling that everything is in sync and flowing smoothly. *How well team members align with this shared Core Identity determines how well they will tap into their Foundations of Greatness.* In addition, we will share that when these components are understood and honored, flow will come faster for your organization.

The Key Enablers of Sustainable Success

Your Core Identity

- a set of Guiding Principles – a compass for all decision-making; define how a team works best together
- a Purpose – why we do our daily work
- a Vision – what we hope our daily work will make possible in the future

Reinforcing Systems

Reinforcing Systems are the purposeful, disciplined practices that reinforce the Core Identity. They are the guardrails that remind us of what we look like when at our best. Reinforcing Systems promote dialogue that leads to ongoing clarification of the boundaries of the Core Identity for all in the organization, and the culture gets stronger. Reinforcing Systems warrant their own chapter, Chapter 4 - Reinforcing Sustainable Success.

Your Core Identity Enables Flow

We work with organizations to create an energizing flow that leads to sustainable success in their daily work life. The key to this process is revealing their unique, intrinsic, energizing Core Identity. During the Culture Clarification process, we bring team members from every part of the organization together to share stories of the organization at its best. These stories surface the organization's energizing *Purpose, Vision,* and *Guiding Principles*. In most cases, we are not asking the organization to become something it has never been but rather to honor what has already enabled them to perform at Peak Performance. That conduct and decision-making become the expected standard moving forward.

Culture Clarification is the first step in the shift from *me* to *team* as team members realize they have experienced Peak Performance in their work together. It becomes energizing for them to understand what they have achieved together and envision what they can do in the future. It is the first step on the journey toward sustainable greatness.

After revealing and clarifying the organization's Core Identity, we assist them in creating and implementing systems that will reinforce their unique and disciplined Core Identity—to reinforce their culture at its best.

Five Stages of Organizational Flow

Like any group of individuals coming together to achieve a goal, organizations go through five stages of culture alignment to reach sustainable flow for success. In the first stage, it's just about each individual and what they want to accomplish for their personal gain. Then, as trust and caring build over time, the members begin to think about the needs of others in the organization. As the organization evolves, the members think about the sustainability of the community they are building. Ultimately, it's not just about individual wants; it is about the team.

As you read about the Five Stages of Organizational Flow, where do you think your organization is? What would it take to move to the next stage?

Stage I – A Community of Independent Contractors

The organization shares a name, but the members operate independently. There is no need for them to work together. They are under the same umbrella but do not interact in service of each other. They are independent operators.

Stages of Organizational Flow

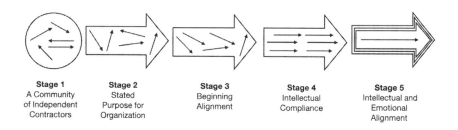

Stage 1	Stage 2	Stage 3	Stage 4	Stage 5
A Community of Independent Contractors	Stated Purpose for Organization	Beginning Alignment	Intellectual Compliance	Intellectual and Emotional Alignment

Stage II - Stated Shared Purpose for the Organization

The team members have a shared name and have clarified a shared Purpose for being, but they continue to work independently. They work in isolated silos, some serving the identified Purpose, but there is no shared compelling Purpose.

Stage III – Beginning Alignment

Now there is a name, a Purpose, and an understanding of how the members of the organization work at their best together. However, some continue to operate as independent contractors in their silos. The necessary Reinforcing Systems are not in place.

Stage IV – Intellectual Compliance

All are on the team seeking the same goals but doing so individually. They are keeping score, competing inside the organization.

Stage V – Intellectual and Emotional Alignment

All are on one team seeking the same goals, collaboratively supporting each other, enabling energizing flow for sustainable success. The goal is for the team to win, regardless of the role each plays to make that possible.

Can you see your organization or any of the communities you belong to in these stages?

The First Two Core Identity Components: A Compelling Purpose and Vision

> Once expanded to the dimensions of more significant ideas, the mind never returns to its original size.
>
> —RALPH WALDO EMERSON

What does it feel like when the team functions at Peak Performance as a unit, when people seem intrinsically energized to be at work, and when the shift from *me* to *team* is in full effect?

It feels like the team is both fueled by energy and creating it, and the energy is contagious.

If there is a market for your product, having a culture that honors your Core Identity is the most significant enabler of success. A Core Identity rooted in a deep and meaningful Purpose can energize teams to thrive far into the future. What motivates us for the short term? What deep and meaningful Purpose will have the potential to energize us day after day? What do we mean by a *deep* and *meaningful* Purpose?

Why does a compelling *Vision* for a better future for its team members, its clients/customers/patients, and its community have the power to energize an organization for generations?

Energized by Our Purpose and Vision

In his book *Start with Why*, Simon Sinek shares that our emotions and feelings emanate from our brains, and they control how we act. We use a simplified description of the brain's two parts for ease of understanding and teaching. Our *primitive brain* is emotionally reactive and designed to protect us; it is about our feelings. Our reactive decision-making resides here. When something feels right or good, or feels wrong or bad, it is our primitive brain guiding our feelings.

We think strategically, collaboratively, and thoughtfully for tomorrow with our *executive brain*. In split seconds, the executive brain informs our primitive brain that the bang that startles us is not a gunshot. Instead, it was the kids slamming the door as they came home from school. If we are open to learning and growing, the executive brain teaches and trains the primitive brain over time to understand real threats.

The feelings from our daily purposeful work and the Vision of a better tomorrow we are creating energize us. These feelings reside in our primitive brain and guide us even under pressure to honor the shared Core Identity that provides safety and security for our community.

Our *executive brain* helps train our *primitive brain* to be more aware of feelings that emanate from purposeful actions to pursue successful sustainability. The threats we face are not of the same magnitude as those confronting our ancestors, but we process them with the primitive brain developed for those threats; therefore, new, more purposeful habits can take time.

The way we treat each other impacts how we feel. Are we valued for our contribution, are we respected for the person we are, and are we in a safe place where we are encouraged to find new and better ways to do our work? Understanding how we work best together enables leaders to tap into the team's collective energy. That energy, once tapped into, can be generative and sustainable.

From a conversation with Bob Sutherland of Cherry Republic on a compelling Purpose and Vision:

I had just finished speaking to a Vistage/TEC Group in Petoskey, Michigan, and was about to drive to Traverse City when Bob Sutherland, the CEO of Cherry Republic, asked to join me. As we drove, I asked about his business. In explaining why he had started the Cherry Republic thirty years earlier, Bob said, "People did not appreciate cherries and the cherry farmers that work so hard to provide them for us."

To secure the future of this important Michigan commodity and the livelihoods of the cherry farmers, he felt he had to do something. Bob opened a store that sold only cherry products—everything from jams and pies to barbecue sauce and cherrywood cutting boards. As of 2022, Cherry Republic has six stores and a mail-order business that ships 100,000+ orders annually, powered by 600 passionate employees who care about sending the world a message about the goodness of cherries.

Our Motivation: Our Four Stages of Fulfillment

Living a Fulfilled, Meaningful Life, True to Our Purpose and Vision

Each of us is energized by various needs and desires, both short term and long term. Bob Sutherland of Cherry Republic had the gratification of seeing cherries appreciated by customers today and the long-term satisfaction of enabling the increased future viability of Michigan's cherry farmers.

Influenced by Fr. Robert Spitzer's "Four Levels of Happiness" and a behavioral assessment used by my mentor, Don McMillan, our team at FS/A created the *Four Stages of Fulfillment*. Its simplicity resonates with clients, and we hope it resonates with you. The Four Stages of Fulfillment is a framework for understanding the motivation behind what we do daily—the *why* behind what we do. The challenge: Are we strategic, and are we purposeful?

Understanding the Four Stages of Fulfillment helps us understand why people behave the way they do in any given situation. The Four Stages of Fulfillment are critical to the Culture Clarification process. We must articulate a clear Core Identity, one that digs much deeper and reaches much higher than the production of products for short-term success.

Our work in guiding clients through the Culture Clarification process confirms this. When four or more people are allowed to come together to reflect and engage on what most motivates them in their work and their lives, they make exceptional decisions for the team. They end up honoring a Purpose and Vision that reflect a *natural desire to pursue fulfillment in the service of others, and to create a better future for their team members, their families, and their communities, all in pursuit of greater safety and security for each other.*

As we mature, we are naturally fulfilled by the higher stages of fulfillment. However, we do see some team members maturing much earlier than others. And as we go through our day, we shift among our four stages of fulfillment. Our challenge is to be mindful of which stage of fulfillment, listed below, we are in and learn to be strategically purposeful.

- Stage I Fulfillment: Meeting Our Primary Physical Needs
- Stage II Fulfillment: Learning, Growing, and Competing
- Stage III Fulfillment: Benefiting Others
- Stage IV Fulfillment: Creating a Better Tomorrow

As you gain a deeper understanding of the Four Stages of Fulfillment, you will see that we help organizations identify their Stage III Fulfillment (Benefiting Others) in their Purpose statement. Their Vision statement is grounded in Stage IV Fulfillment (Creating a Better Tomorrow).

Making the Connection to Our Life's Purpose

When we are "doing," we receive short-term energy through stress hormones like adrenaline, cortisol, and dopamine. Supportive in small doses, they push and prepare us to act, they drive us to meet our primary needs and feel a sense of physical and emotional fulfillment.

Over time, if we are doing the right things for the long term, we feel greater safety and security. We then feel the effects of what some call the "happiness hormones"—the stress blockers oxytocin and serotonin. We get to appreciate the sacrifices we have made, and the delayed gratification required to create the safety and security of today. We feel the benefits of strategic, purposeful thinking and acting, and we can become motivated to continue this intentional and purposeful life.

We understand it isn't easy to stop and consider why we are doing what we do—or always connect it to our life's purpose. We see the discomfort we create when we ask others why they are doing what they do. It's easy to become accustomed and desensitized to the toll that endorphins, dopamine, and adrenaline take on us as they keep us in motion. We don't stop and think about *why* we do what we do, even when it may not be feeling right. We don't reflect on these feelings. We in America take great pride in putting our nose to the grindstone. And we get about *taking action and staying busy.* We are energized by checking off items on our to-do list—we keep on moving. We are wired for short-term gratification!

We present the Four Stages of Fulfillment to clients as an invitation to step away from the stress-cycle of doing. Instead, think about our motivations and their impact on our energy, lives, and health. This may be the most challenging part of the journey. Stop, think, and ask, "Why am I doing what I am doing, and how does it connect to what is most meaningful to me?"

After the first day of a two-day retreat in Chicago on Unleashing Your Foundation of Greatness, one of the participants exclaimed, "We have no idea what you are talking about!" He was confused about the challenge to take time—time he did not feel they had—to think about the motivation behind what they were doing. He was part of a group of twenty leaders who had asked me to share how they could find greater flow in their work. He was confused; he did not have enough time in the day to address all the needs of his clients, his staff, and himself.

After the second day, it was like a light went on for all of them. You could see each of them slowing down and reflecting on this issue: "Why do I think we will achieve more if I am busy?"

Stage I Fulfillment: Meeting Our Primary Physical Needs

We are born into the world seeking Stage I Fulfillment. When a baby is cold, wet, tired, or hungry, it cries. A baby is happy for a few hours at best; then, the cycle begins again.

The Four Stages of Development

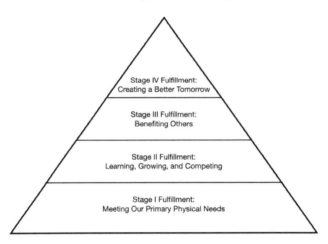

Stage IV Fulfillment:
Creating a Better Tomorrow

Stage III Fulfillment:
Benefiting Others

Stage II Fulfillment:
Learning, Growing, and Competing

Stage I Fulfillment:
Meeting Our Primary Physical Needs

Stage I Fulfillment, and the satisfaction it creates, is short term, but we must meet our primary needs or perish. Eating, sleeping, and seeking comfort, warmth, and safety—the better we care for ourselves physically, the better chance we have of surviving and thriving. Thus, Stage I Fulfillment can be viewed as the base of the pyramid—it better prepares us for our upward journey to experience the other three Stages of Fulfillment. The better we care for our physical and emotional well-being, the stronger the foundation we possess to serve the higher stages of fulfillment.

Stuck at Stage I Fulfillment

Those fixated on Stage I Fulfillment become consumed with themselves and are not concerned with their impact on others. These individuals cannot delay gratification, which compromises their preparedness to go to a higher stage of fulfillment. They are stuck, and they lack the maturity to delay gratification.

As adults, we are all in constant negotiation with our Four Stages of Fulfillment. There is a natural pull to meet our primary Stage I Fulfillment needs. However, how much personal attention do we need to effectively move to Stage II Fulfillment so that we can learn, compete, and win? How much sleep, food, drink, and medications are purposeful?

Stage I Fulfillment Attributes

- The primary impact is on oneself.
- Understanding begins at birth.
- Behavior includes fulfilling the basic needs for food, water, and sleep, and dressing or setting the thermostat for comfort.
- Fulfillment begins immediately and lasts for hours.
- This stage is vital for survival.
- Exemplars include infants, who come into the world at Stage I. You may know people whose Stage I Fulfillment needs are like gravity, constantly pulling on them.

Stage I Fulfillment is about our immediate needs with or without considering how it impacts our ability to compete at Stage II Fulfillment.

Stage II Fulfillment: Learning, Growing, and Competing

Each stage builds on the previous stage. When our primary needs have been met, and we mature, we seek Stage II Fulfillment to compete with and compare ourselves to others. We begin to understand Stage II Fulfillment in early adolescence. We desire a foundation for independence, and we learn and grow to pave our path to survive and flourish. We begin to compare ourselves to others regarding knowledge, achievements, and possessions. We never lose our ego, so we are all competitors throughout our lifetime. At Stage II, we pursue fulfillment by building our competencies to survive, achieve, and succeed. We may attain advanced degrees or pursue athletic or creative excellence. We compare our performance to that of others. We strive for more significant signs of accomplishment with compensation, titles, and recognition. While trying to become the best we can be, we build a strong base of competencies to serve us on our life's journey.

With increased competency, we take on more significant challenges and can achieve more success. If we choose to direct our competency for the greater good, the process of seeking Stage II Fulfillment sets the foundation for making a positive impact on the world. But it can be hurtful too.

Stuck at Stage II Fulfillment

As accomplishments bring recognition, some are lured into the short-term satisfaction of seeking prestige, status, and money for themselves above all else. Their ego can blindly drive them to compare their success to others', and they see the accumulation of material goods as a sign that they are winning.

American entrepreneur Martin Shkreli had tremendous financial success and seemed to have a stellar career when he founded Turing Pharmaceuticals in early 2015. However, he earned widespread contempt in an arrogant pursuit of windfall profits when, as demand surged, he increased the price of an anti-malarial drug by more than 5,000%. By the fall of 2015, he had been indicted for securities fraud.

There may be no greater disaster that exemplified the fixation on Stage II Fulfillment than the compensation systems in the American mortgage industry from 2004 to 2010. Mortgage loan officers and their superiors were rewarded handsomely when they sold harmful mortgage products to thousands of unsuspecting clients. The results hurt the clients, the stockholders, and, ultimately, the mortgage company and the entire nation. The shock of that recession, a result of their short-term reward systems, will take generations to move past.

The joy of Stage II Fulfillment and the energy it creates is fleeting, but it is vital to building a competent and robust foundation. While growing and becoming more competent is critical, living a life in service at this stage is a no-win proposition. Someone else will always know more, have more, or do more, which can lead to feeling behind in the game, and always defeated.

Stage II Attributes Fulfillment

- The primary impact is ego gratification.
- Understanding begins in early adolescence.
- Behaviors and experiences include learning, growing, getting better, and being more competent, with an emphasis on short-term accomplishment. It can be showy if one is ego-centric and seeking prestige.
- The fulfillment begins right away and lasts a short time, perhaps months.
- It is significant for building our competencies and confidence; it provides a strong base of skills and knowledge.
- The exemplars are gifted athletes, musicians, scientists, lottery winners, game show winners, and those with oversized houses, cars, and titles.

Those who stop maturing and seek to win at this stage show their success and want all to know how accomplished they are. Those who continue to mature use the competencies built at Stage II to benefit others at Stage III.

Stage III Fulfillment: Benefiting Others

Stage III Fulfillment is sought by mature individuals who feel a strong sense of responsibility for the welfare of others. We see some young people demonstrating advanced maturity in the service of others. We see college students showing signs of maturity in choosing to study professions like teaching and medicine to serve their communities.

Most of us begin to be motivated to live our lives by helping others around ages twenty-five to thirty-five.

In Stage III Fulfillment, satisfaction comes from supporting and enabling others to accomplish and succeed. Efforts as a parent, coach, or mentor may not yield fruit right away—it can take years or decades for the benefits of our efforts to be realized. Regardless of the outcome, the people being supported feel cared for right away, helping them feel like they belong, are being looked after, and are safe. This generates the hormones serotonin and oxytocin, resulting in feelings of contentment. Those doing the supporting work feel the positive impact of their intentions, and they feel they are contributing to the benefit of another. They, too, receive the benefits of oxytocin and serotonin when they support others. The good feelings from this process make it easier for mature individuals to continue to support others. The energy at Stage III Fulfillment can become generative.

Ari Weinzweig, one of the founding partners in the legendary Zingerman's Family of Businesses in Ann Arbor, provided an example of Stage III Fulfillment one day when I was at lunch with one of our clients. Our client owned hotels and restaurants, and we wanted him to experience the flow that comes from the shift from *me* to *team* Zingerman's exemplifies. Ari came over and asked how our lunch was, and he proceeded to remove our dishes and wipe the table. When I shared that the busser was one of the founding partners of an organization with more than $65 million in sales, my client refused to believe it. This team-focused approach begins with leadership and permeates Zingerman's because of exemplary Stage III leadership.

Having a Purpose that contributes to the benefit of others is critical in creating the energy needed for sustainable success, as a team, in business and life. Stage III Fulfillment utilizes the competencies built in Stage II but uses them in the service of others.

Stage III Fulfillment Attributes

- The primary impact is on others.

- Our understanding begins most often in adulthood, at ages twenty-five to thirty-five; women tend to get it before men.

- At this stage, we are energized to serve and care for others.

- The fulfillment is delayed, taking hold years after our actions, when the fruits of our labors surface in others, and it lasts years, perhaps decades.

- Work done at this stage is deeply impactful on society.

- The exemplars are police officers, educators, medical professionals, and those who are motivated to see others thrive.

Our sustainable Purpose in life resides in Stage III Fulfillment. You can look to those who have meant the most to you, those you admire and respect in your life, to see their Stage III Fulfillment in action.

Energized by Stage III Fulfillment

We see examples of Stage III Fulfillment in parents becoming responsible for the growth and development of their children. We see it in people who choose to do volunteer work to help others. We see it every time someone steps up to help a neighbor in need. We see it when people organize relief efforts after a natural disaster. We also see it in the way people choose to be of service in their work—regardless of their field. We see employees who consistently choose to support their co-workers. We've encountered workers who see interactions with customers as an opportunity to spread joy. And these people are willing to question leadership when something looks harmful to employees or their customers.

From the CEO of a healthcare device company:

"We had a sales leader who saw everything through the lens of 'What does this mean to me? What will this do for me?' as opposed to 'What is best for the company?' After instituting our Purpose and Guiding Principles, he's shifted and now looks at things from a team perspective . . . he has a much more external/global view of what we're trying to accomplish companywide. You get blinded by revenue and sales, but they might be creating collateral damage along the way. The financial benefit you see initially can be offset by the de-energizing forces they create on the organization."

We help clients reveal the Stage III Fulfillment-focused Purpose of their organization. It can be challenging to explain to some business leaders that working in the service of others is fundamental to building a thriving enterprise. Who can blame them? Classical economic theory has maintained that humans are selfish and, when given a choice, act in their self-interest. This old tenet of economic theory is present as a strand in the DNA of most organizations. Work is set up as a series of quid pro quo arrangements. When we do what is expected of us, we are told that there will be commissions, bonuses, and better pay. Too often, we are set up to compete against co-workers to prove who most deserves to climb the ladder.

This belief in the fundamental selfishness of humans is not backed by science. On the contrary, left to our own devices, we most often act in the best interest of our community. As it turns out, we are not most fulfilled by Stage II motivators, as we've been taught to believe, but by a deep and meaningful service-oriented Purpose. A Purpose reflected in a Stage III pursuit of fulfillment that ultimately leads to Stage IV Fulfillment from creating greater safety and security for our community.

Stage IV Fulfillment: Creating a Better Tomorrow

Whereas Stage III Fulfillment is rooted in the present, Stage IV Fulfillment is about living life with faith in a Vision. This Vision is powered by a belief that our actions today will create a better tomorrow, even though we may not live to see its full realization. Living at the Stage IV Fulfillment level requires a level of maturity that comes in middle age or later for most of us. The actions of the most respected, enduringly successful individuals and organizations are rooted in Stages III and IV Fulfillment: A Purpose that benefits others today (Stage III) in pursuit of a Vision that contributes to a better future (Stage IV).

Stage IV Fulfillment Attributes

- The impact is on future generations.

- The understanding begins at middle age or later, around age fifty or so.

- It is characterized by having faith that one's actions will positively impact the future.

- The fulfillment is ever-present; it is a feeling of contentment in living life with a deeply meaningful Vision.

- It is significant for its lasting positive impact on future generations. This is where the Visions for our life and organization reside.

- The exemplars are researchers who toil for decades in hopes of a breakthrough, and then give their findings away, religious leaders, those in the military who are willing to sacrifice their lives for a better tomorrow, and the rare politician who is thinking about a better future.

Energized by Stage IV Fulfillment

During the Culture Clarification retreat we take clients through, we ask team members to imagine the impact they might have on each other, their community, and the world if they were to work in service of their deep and meaningful Purpose every day. And what if everyone in the organization continued to do so for years, decades, and generations — what picture would that make possible? What impact on their community could they make? This is the most challenging part of our work. Few of us live thinking about "why" we are doing what we do, and it is a challenge our brains are not used to addressing. This difficulty is exemplified by the leader who said, "I do not know what you are talking about!" after the first day of our retreat. We can see in people's eyes that they are feeling the same; few at the retreat genuinely understand what we are talking about. After some time, we progress, and team members inevitably create a picture of a thriving organization, a healthy, thriving community, and a better world. This picture of a better future is the organization's inspiring shared Vision.

Our ability to shift from short-term to long-term thinking is directly aligned with our maturity, which varies from person to person. The good thing is that maturity comes with age, generally!

Story of the Stages of Fulfillment

Seventeenth-century English architect Christopher Wren spoke with the men building St. Paul's Cathedral in London, which he had designed. "What are you doing?" he asked. One man replied, "I am cutting a piece of stone." Another said, "I am earning five shillings two pence a day." The third said, "I am helping Sir Christopher Wren build a beautiful cathedral." The first two were living and thinking about Stage II Fulfillment. The third had a Vision at Stage IV Fulfillment, which is more motivating and inspiring, enabling Peak Performance to occur more naturally.

Everything We Do Should Be in Service of Our Vision

Humans are wired to be busy. Being busy is natural and effortless, but being productive and purposeful takes conscious effort until it becomes a habit. There is immediate personal gratification from being busy, so why slow down?

The visioning part of the Culture Clarification retreat connects what we are doing to what we are making possible—we are creating a Vision of what can be. An inspiring Vision captures our imagination and energizes us. *What* we do may not be motivating, but *why* we do it can be.

Swiss Watchmakers

By the 1960s, Swiss watchmaking had dominated watch manufacturing and sales for more than 100 years. In 1968, the Swiss had 65% of the market share and 80% of profits from watches. That year Swiss researchers invented the quartz-crystal watch, which was battery-operated and used fewer moving parts. Though they created it, Swiss watchmakers refused to adopt the new technology. They could not envision future watches that did not feature their superior mechanical beauty. Instead, the Japanese company Seiko bought the technology. By 1980, Swiss watchmakers had laid off 50,000 of their 65,000 workers. The demand for quartz-crystal watches had cut into the demand for their mechanical movement watches. Swiss watchmakers were guided by the *how* of their work, not the *why* of their Vision for their business.

The Newspaper Industry

There was a time when newspapers dominated information sharing through their print editions. They became experts at printing paper around the country to meet readers' needs. They continually increased the capital assets needed to provide more paper more efficiently. As the advent of electronic media began to fulfill the information needs of readers, most newspaper companies failed to adjust. As a result, once-powerful community presences are mostly gone, not because the service they provided was no longer needed but because of how they provided it.

It is easy for us to get caught up in the *what* and *how* of our doing—we are wired to do. What is needed is a connection to *why* we are doing it. What Purpose are we serving today to make what Vision possible tomorrow?

How Visions Become Reality—The Reticular Activating System

Luck is what happens when preparation meets opportunity.

—ROMAN PHILOSOPHER SENECA

What happens in life is not as random as we may believe, and what we think about makes all the difference. Strategically and purposefully managing our thinking, like having a vision of a desired future, gives us a better chance of that future becoming a reality.

As we learn to envision a positive future, we open ourselves to gathering the information needed to get there. We become less concerned about where the information comes from—or who delivers it. We become less concerned with *the way things have always been done*. We are more open to creative and novel approaches to move us toward our vision more quickly. We seek input from unlikely sources, and in so doing, we become more attuned listeners, more likely to see the strengths of others and the value of collaboration to reach our destination.

The brain's reticular activating system (RAS) is working behind the scenes, subconsciously, to help guide us on our journey. By visualizing the desired destination, we prepare our RAS to act as a radar to collect data to aid us on our path to that destination. Our mind is open to information that can help us, and it sorts through the information chaos to identify data that can help us move toward our vision.

Our RAS allows us to find a better path to where we want to go. And it works to steer us clear of anything that takes us off the path. Without us consciously knowing it, our RAS is guiding our choices. The clearer the vision of the desired destination, the better our RAS can do its job.

While we consciously create the vision, the RAS works subconsciously to identify pathways toward it. When these pathways lead to success, we may call it luck, but it is not luck. It began with a vision we created and actions based on the information filtered by our RAS.

Here is a personal experience that made me believe in the power of a positive vision. I keep a regular to-do list and take pride in checking off my accomplishments. This works well, but at some point, I began to get frustrated with the lack of progress on larger goals. I decided to create a new list to address this issue. I started my *Top-Ten Life To-Do's*. It was a list of the most meaningful goals to me in my lifetime. Near the top of the list was a home renovation. I wrote:

Home Renovation - To have a home that is so warm and welcoming that our children and grandchildren love being here and cannot wait to come back to spend more time with us.

The setting of our home is spectacular; it sits on a bluff overlooking the Huron River in Ann Arbor. However, after moving in, I was in the beginning stages at FS/A, and we were not financially able to do the much-needed renovations. We felt certain a remodel would only be possible far in the future.

After writing this goal down, we decided to see what kind of budget we would need to fund the renovation. At that time, I overheard someone say they had just gotten a crazy-low interest rate refinancing their home. Then, I ran into my banker by chance and asked him about refinancing. We increased our mortgage for part of the renovation while not increasing our payments. Seemingly out of nowhere, we had a big part of our funding. We had an architect draw some concepts, and we regularly tore pictures from magazines that depicted the ambiance we were seeking. The image of our finished project was becoming more and more apparent. Meanwhile, business at FS/A took off at the same time, and we now had the finances to pay for the renovation. The picture was clear, and the RAS did its job such that eighteen months after making renovation #1 on my *Top-Ten Life To-Do's*, we unbelievably had the home of our dreams.

The Third Core Identity Component: Guiding Principles for Working at Our Best Together

An organization striving to unleash its greatness is energized by its meaningful *Purpose* today as it works toward an inspirational *Vision* of a better tomorrow. The organization's *Guiding Principles*—the third enabler in the Core Identity—will illustrate how members achieve Peak Performance together.

Surveys and interviews we conduct with our clients reveal many Guiding Principles. They surface in the stories where team members have embodied principles (or values) listed below like *trust, caring, fairness, curiosity, innovation, teamwork*, etc. We help surface the four or five Guiding Principles they find most compelling. These principles surfaced in how they achieved Peak Performance in the past and will guide team members as a standard for working together moving forward.

Leadership at a healthcare organization felt they kept "hiring the wrong people" and asked for our help. There seemed to be excellent people on the team, but the energy and morale were not good. We helped them clarify their Guiding Principles, and they started holding each other responsible for living to that standard. A key leader departed because he could not thrive in this garden with the new standards. The organization as a whole, however, was energized by the new standards for working together. Those who stayed experienced a transformation for the better to an extent they had never dreamt possible. The positive energy flowed. The new hiring process, which included assessment for fit with the Core Identity, brought in team members that fit right away, making the organization even better. The transformational change was fast, and the organization continues to flourish today.

Popular Guiding Principles

Abundance	Fairness	Mentoring
Adaptable	Family	Openness
Authenticity	Flexible	Persistence
Balance	Fun	Positivity
Beauty	Generosity	Professional
Caring	Genuineness	Reliable
Collaboration	Growing	Resilient
Commitment	Honesty	Respect
Compassion	Humility	Responsibility
Courage	Innovation	Responsiveness
Creativity	Integrity	Team/Teamwork
Dedication	Kindness	Transparency
Determination	Learning	Trust
Empathy	Loyalty	
Entrepreneurship	Love	

Guiding Principles—What They Do

- They guide decision-making on a personal and organizational level.
- They help clarify relationship boundaries.
- They heighten awareness about how we're treating each other.
- They give a common language for discussing interpersonal conflict.
- They give a common language for discussing organizational and systemic issues.
- They guide us in our learning, growing, and teaching.
- They identify how/what leadership will address with rewards and questions.
- They label intrinsic feelings.
- They require no external explanation (goes to the limbic brain; it feels right).

Note that Guiding Principles are not operating practices, business strategies, or competencies. They are not adjustable in response to the market or for different constituencies. They are our "how" we conduct ourselves at all times.

The Role of Feelings and Our Guiding Principles

Each of us possesses an internal set of Guiding Principles that govern how we respond under pressure, whether we are conscious of it or not. When honored or violated, these principles determine how we feel. This is no less true at work than in any other aspect of our lives.

There is a natural flow when we are operating in alignment with our shared principles. Even in our struggles and challenges, we feel confident as we journey toward success. We feel we were put in this place to positively impact something much bigger than ourselves. These feelings are real. They rise in response to the release of our happiness hormones, serotonin and oxytocin. They are also stress blockers, and they allow us to tap into our energy for Peak Performance.

Those who try to help others feel secure and successful also receive the benefits of oxytocin and serotonin. The positive feelings they experience assist them in continuing their efforts to support others. This energy is natural, and it's generative. This is how collaboration and teamwork make sustainable success possible.

When our principles are violated, we feel the effects of adrenaline, dopamine, and cortisol—stress hormones that may lead to feelings of frustration, sadness, anger, isolation, jealousy, etc. These feelings are primal and de-energizing. The long-term effects of too much adrenaline and cortisol can shorten life spans. At the very least, when our principles are violated, the negative feelings hinder our capacity to address the task at hand. Over time, anyone experiencing these feelings can negatively impact the team's potential. In the extreme, the frustration of having one's principles regularly violated can lead to the team breaking apart.

Leadership's job is to do everything possible to ensure that Guiding Principles are reinforced and honored, so that team members feel safe and secure and positioned for Peak Performance. The reward for creating this alignment that creates a natural flow goes beyond the financial impact: It becomes life-sustaining.

Leadership's Sensitivity to Feelings

With the score tied and seconds remaining, Rumeal Robinson went to the line in the final seconds of the NCAA Basketball National Championship game with a chance to win it for Michigan. The opposing coach called a time-out to increase the pressure on Rumeal. Michigan's Coach Steve Fisher sensed the tension all felt in the moment and had compassion for what Rumeal was experiencing. To relieve the stress, he said something funny, animating the entire huddle with laughter. Rumeal made the two free throws, and Michigan won the National Championship.

In their first year as a varsity sport, I had a similar experience with the Michigan Women's Soccer Team. In the first game of the Big Ten Championships, we were seeded last in the conference, and we were playing #1 seeded Penn State, who had won the conference championship the year before. Surprisingly, we tied Penn State and went into overtime. Overtime victories are determined by a shootout where each team pits one player against the opposing goalie for seven chances to score.

In the huddle preparing for the shootout, Michigan's Coach Deb Belkin could sense the pressure on the team. Like Coach Fisher, she said something that created laughter, reducing the tension of the moment and re-emphasizing being team members in support of each other. The pressure in the Penn State huddle was clear to all observers: they could not believe they were in this situation! You can guess what happened. Michigan beat Penn State. One team performed to their capability; the other did not. Did leadership play a role at a critical time?

Being sensitive and caring about what your team is feeling directly correlates to Peak Performance, the objective of leadership.

One Client's Shared Guiding Principles

Respect   *We honor the integrity of individual lives.*

Dedication   *Our resilience and professionalism are demonstrated by our commitment and hard work.*

Integrity   *We build trust through credibility and responsibility.*

Teamwork   *Through communication and collaboration, we work together as one.*

Positivity   *We create opportunities from our mistakes and celebrate our successes.*

Two Essential Guiding Principles: Trust and Caring

The two Guiding Principles we have found in enduringly successful organizations are trust (*honesty, integrity, responsibility*) and caring (*love, respect, empathy, compassion*). These principles are fundamental to lasting relationships. Sustainable success is not possible without them, whether in a couple, an athletic team, or an organization.

Trust is about consistently and responsibly doing the right thing. *Caring* is about demonstrating that we value the health and welfare of each other and the organization that is our lifeblood.

Including these two in the organization's shared Guiding Principles is not an option—human nature demands it.

Trust

Here is an example of trusting in employees that occurred in the aftermath of the 9/11 attacks. Airlines in the US saw a steep drop in business as many individuals and organizations avoided flying. Like their competitors, management at Southwest Airlines, led by Herb Kelleher, faced tough questions: *"How do we reduce our costs by 40% to stay in business? People are not flying; what are our options?"* Southwest's management included employees as part of the team crafting the answer; they made the required expense cuts with the team's input without laying off any employees. Not only did they survive, but they thrived when people began to fly again. Southwest got back to profitability faster than any other airline. Research by Kim Cameron, David Whetten, Jody Hoffer Gittell, and others illustrated the direct correlation between team ownership in cost reductions and recovery. Southwest remains in business today, while several of its competitors from 2001 who chose top-down authoritarian decision-making went out of business or were absorbed by other airlines. Kelleher understood that building trust with your people is critical for sustainable success.

When We Lose Trust

After twenty-one years at Michigan Athletics, I was two years into being co-owner of a small startup company; we manufactured leather for suppliers to the automotive industry. It was an ugly time in the automotive industry when purchasing agents for manufacturers were rewarded for painful concessions from suppliers, and they were beating us up in pricing negotiations. One day, I had a confrontation with one of the purchasing agents. He told me, "Your entire shipment of leather, every square foot has defects." They had already received a 15% discount to begin using our product when at the end of our long conversation, he said, "OK, give us another 10% discount, and we will use it."

If "every square foot is defective," how could he use it? I knew I was in the wrong business; I had no interest in partnering with people willing to sell their integrity for personal gain. I left to start the best job I have ever had, teaching the enablers of sustainable success to leaders.

Caring

A client with the Guiding Principle of caring hired a homeless person who kept begging for a chance to prove himself. He became a role model, and the company created an annual award in his name, honoring their team member with the greatest work ethic.

The prototype of the leader as someone who must be hard driving and charismatic is not correct. Just as they do for each team member, the components for sustainable success apply to leaders. In service of a Purpose that serves others, the Guiding Principles of caring and mutual trust are not optional.

Great leaders who succeed over time build trusting and respectful relationships with team members who go the extra mile for the team.

Build Trust and Caring with Actions

Trust is closely tied to caring. Some people do not distinguish between them because they generate similar feelings. Trust is built on taking responsibility for being there the way you said you would be, while caring is a feeling that comes from someone showing kindness or concern for us. Great leaders reinforce their words: They do what they say. There may be no greater need in human nature than the feeling that you can trust someone who deeply cares about you. We feel safe, secure, and valued.

Great leaders demonstrate that caring and trust are parts of their being by:

- humbly taking time to get to know others, to know them deeply;
- recognizing that there is a Foundation of Greatness in each team member to be tapped into, honored, and built upon;

- being unafraid to use the word *love* when expressing how they feel about their team;
- building caring and trusting relationships that put the other person's needs first;
- recognizing that caring and trust are two-way commitments that must be transparent;
- recognizing that caring and trust are both at the core of enabling safety and security, which all human beings seek;
- demonstrating to team members that the leader has their back;
- supporting team members who need to find a better fit elsewhere;
- letting team members know they are each cared about.

Trust and Caring Exemplified

Jim Richardson, twenty-seven years head coach of the University of Michigan Women's Swimming and Diving team, is one of those leaders I studied to understand the differentiators of exceptional leaders. Jim built a team on mutual trust of and caring for each other. Swimming is scored on individual performance. Regardless of the external variables, it is just the swimmer and the clock. (Some ask if this should be considered a team sport.)

There was a team ethos, even though it was up to each swimmer individually to compete. This ethos guided them to be one team on the same page in service of each other. Jim's respect for their commitment to being the best they could, not just for themselves but for the team, generated his deep trust that they would do the right thing under pressure. One year, the NCAA Championships tested this ethos under the most extraordinary pressure possible in intercollegiate athletics.

Jim came down with the flu and spent most of the National Championship in his hotel room, isolated from the team. Meanwhile, the team had built this trust in each other and deep care for each other;

each team member knew her back was covered. Whatever happened, they were there for each other unconditionally, with or without their coach.

Thus far in the history of the NCAA Women's Swimming and Diving Championships, the same three teams finished in the top three spots, and Michigan was not one of them. However, this year, Michigan was in second place after the first day and then again #2 after the second day. On the third day, it came down to the final event of the meet with the National Championship, the platform dive, on the line. Stanford was #1, and Michigan was #2. Michigan had beaten Stanford in the tower dive earlier in the year. Those were the points that would make Michigan the National Champions. However, Michigan's diver was competing internationally at the Pan Am Games that weekend and was not at the meet.

Stanford won the championship with their tower dive. What happened next exemplified what a team built on trust and caring for each other can do. They had done the best they could, and they were joyous! They sang so loud and danced so long while celebrating their second-place finish that they delayed the presentation of the National Championship trophy. They believed in each other, cared about each other, and did the best they could. They were champions; they were all they could be that day for each other.

Clarifying the Boundaries of Our Guiding Principles

Organizations may share similar Guiding Principles. However, the boundaries of acceptability for each Guiding Principle will uniquely define each organization. Through ongoing storytelling, reflection, and discussion, the organization clarifies which behaviors are *in bounds* and which are *out-of-bounds* for each Guiding Principle. The Guiding Principles are evolving, crystallizing, and deepening in meaning as they grow in the hearts and minds of each team member.

Our Need for Boundaries

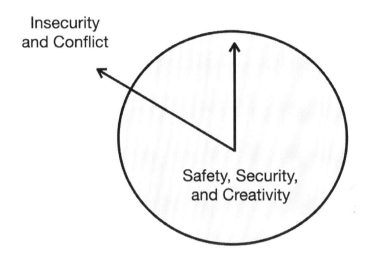

Insecurity and Conflict

Safety, Security, and Creativity

The process of clarifying boundaries of the Guiding Principles is a never-ending journey; it is human nature to test the boundaries to find safety and security. This is the responsibility of leadership. Old habits die hard, and it is leadership's responsibility to consistently reinforce the boundaries. We all have habits we need to change! Over time, when confronted with tough decisions, the exemplary stories team members remember guide their decision-making. This is how you create greater alignment and flow for the organization. Through illustrative storytelling, the boundaries of your Guiding Principles will become instinctive. Then, through our feelings, we make decisions in the organization's best interest. Naturally, the organic flow has started.

Cheering on individuals playing the game in-bounds and addressing out-of-bounds behavior is a fundamental responsibility of leadership. We will address Reinforcing Systems later in the book to help clarify systems you can implement for all to understand your unique boundaries.

Questions to Consider

- Is our organization's Core Identity clear to all team members?
- Are we referencing our Purpose, Vision, and Guiding Principles frequently?
- How do I feel and how do our team members feel about our alignment to Peak Performance?
- Are we telling stories of "at our best" in service of Peak Performance?

Chapter Takeaways

- A clear Core Identity honors the organization and supports its sustainability.
- At any time, be mindful about which stage of fulfillment we are in and decide if it is appropriate.
- Our feelings tell us our alignment with what we should be when performing at Peak Performance.
- Our feelings are tied to honoring our Core Identity.
- Trust and caring are two Guiding Principles that are imperative for sustainability.

CHAPTER 3

CULTURE CLARIFICATION: REVEALING THE GREATNESS THAT RESIDES IN YOUR ORGANIZATION

We have become the firm we all left twenty-eight years ago! Can you help us get back to who we desire to be?

—FOUNDING PARTNER
of a large and prestigious law firm

There is a process for organizations to reveal what they have looked like at their best. The result is a standard for future sustainably successful decision-making.

Team members from all levels of the organization come together for their Culture Clarification retreat, which typically lasts one or two days. We have told them that this retreat will be their opportunity to begin the process of solidifying the foundation of the organization, of clarifying a Core Identity that will guide the organization's work far into the future. Team member attitudes range from eagerness to engage to a complete lack of trust. These attitudes are the result of their past experiences in the organization.

For those whose experiences have been less than positive, can they trust that we will respect their experiences? Can they trust that this meeting will make a difference? Will it be any different from the flavor-of-the-month teachings of the past?

They will not have to wait to see that trust and caring are honored. They are about to experience a leadership team that listens empathetically as team members tell stories of the organization at its best.

Each team member—including each leader—casts one vote to decide the components of the organization's Purpose, Vision, and Guiding Principles. It's a democratic process that shifts the power of responsibility from a leadership team to all organization members. The result is a clear responsibility of each individual to honor the organization's Peak Performance culture. The shift from *me* to *team* has begun.

Preparing the Team

Surveys and Interviews

Leading up to the retreat, we conduct surveys, followed by interviews that reveal how team members view the organization, how they feel about their lives at work, and how they feel about the effectiveness of themselves, their team members, and leadership. They reveal what has worked in the past, what is working now, and what needs to improve. They often point to frustration with leadership and the state of the organization. These feelings are resident in the organization. Now leadership knows, sometimes for the first time.

The stated lack of satisfaction with the status quo indicates that team members care. They want the organization to be better, and they want the organization to value their contribution. They want to contribute to and feel a part of a thriving team, something all humans desire.

Often, the request for input at the retreat is the team member's first opportunity to be heard by leadership. And it's the first opportunity for the thoughts and feelings of the team to be genuinely valued. This is an opportunity for the team to feel cared about and respected. We often hear, *"I feel fortunate to work for a company that respects my thoughts and cares enough to ask me about them and then listens to what I have to say."*

Here is a sample of questions from the Organizational Culture Survey:

- What attracted you to this company?
- What are the company's greatest strengths?
- What stories would you tell new employees to help them understand the company *at its best?*
- Provide examples of violations of what you feel the company should stand for (no names).
- What difference in the world do we hope to make?
- What values best represent the company?

In one case, responses to the survey revealed an organization that once had a prestigious legacy in the community as a great place to work with great pay and caring ownership. One employee shared, *"When my dad went to pay the hospital bill after my brother was born, he was told that the company's president had already paid it."* We heard many stories like this. It wasn't just a company but a community pillar.

The survey revealed that the present organization was different. One team member shared, *"When the price of gas goes down, and I can afford to drive farther away, I'll quit this job. With the current gas price, I can't afford to drive anywhere right now."* Other responses exposed maltreatment by management, a lack of engagement and a lack of trust, and a toxic culture where the company's jobs were no longer desirable.

The survey responses—*positive* and *negative*—reveal the components of their Guiding Principles, Purpose, and Vision for the team members to consider at the retreat.

The Team Engagement Process

Before the retreat, we provide all team members with the Core Identity component data from the survey responses. Then, from that report, each team member will have the opportunity to lobby for what they believe should be key components of the Core Identity moving forward. So that they can lobby effectively, we challenge them to surface stories demonstrating the component to support their point. These stories are critical in clarifying their Core Identity.

After the lobbying is done and the stories have been told, each organization member will vote on the Core Identity components: their Guiding Principles, Purpose, and Vision.

Many are energized by the process and what is unfolding. It makes sense to them—for once, we will stand for something! It reinforces that team members are driving this process. *Team members* have been allowed to share their feelings honestly via the survey, interviews, and retreat participation. The survey results—the good, the bad, and the ugly—have been openly shared. And it is *team members* who are given a chance to speak and be respected. They are beginning to feel valued and respected and believe they can create something extraordinary.

Preparing Leadership

In preparation for the Culture Clarification retreat, it is beneficial to coach the leader and the leadership team to understand better who they are personally. We encourage them to step away from the workday rush, stop and breathe, and consider what is most important to them. They must recognize that they each possess their own Core Identity. Challenging the leaders to examine their Core Identity enlightens the organization's journey. This helps create a feeling in the leader that this journey is deep and meaningful, as they tap into who they are meant to be. We ask them to think of the collective energy that can come from an organization tapping into what they are meant to be together! Ultimately, this work will be about energizing the organization by tapping into its deep and meaningful Core Identity.

Attributes of Exceptional Leaders

Our work to build sustainable organizations took us directly to how leaders make their teams feel—do leaders create positive energy in their team? We have found a consistent recipe in leaders who created sustainable and generative organizations. Exceptional leaders possess four fundamental characteristics:

- *curiosity*, with a desire to learn and grow
- *a passion to serve others*
- *authenticity* (by building *trust* with all actions)
- *deep caring* for team members

The Common Thread: Humility

A lifetime of studying leaders of sustainably great organizations, with over two decades of coaching leaders, has revealed that humility is the common thread weaving through these four fundamental attributes.

Exceptional leaders share these common attributes of humility:

- They are humble about what they know and are curious to learn about others' perspectives.
- They feel they are on a journey to becoming extraordinary. As fuzzy as that might look, they are passionate about modeling exceptional characteristics of leaders they admire and are humble about where they are on their journey.

- They are reflective. They know they are biased and limited in what they see, and they understand their perspective is narrow and limited.
- They recognize that human nature is complex and that there may be no absolute *right* way to do something.
- They seek and value diversity of opinions, backgrounds, and perspectives in service of learning and growing together.

Humility enables them to:

- listen, so team members feel heard and respected;
- take the time for others even when they are busy, so people feel valued;
- admit they need others, and recognize their contributions;
- be *vulnerable, which* leads to *authenticity,* which leads to being *trusted;*
- think in terms of what others need, so they feel cared for;
- seek to understand others' perspectives, so they feel respected;
- admit they may be wrong, and seek those who can help, so they can be trusted.

We had the good fortune to work with an exceptional first-time chair of a large academic research department. She came in with tremendous accolades and intellect. Though she had never been a leader of a large unit, she had a vision for the department. With the humility to accept that she didn't know how to get there, she asked for help. She desired to learn and grow to be more effective in leading the department. She was and continues to be a voracious reader, curious about why things work or do not work. She took the department from a financial burden on the university with poor team management to a profitable and high-performing premier role model for employee engagement. Not surprisingly, she is now leading a significantly larger department at another academic research university.

Humility at the Highest Level

President Gerald R. Ford played football at the University of Michigan. An avid supporter of his alma mater, he hosted golf outings for Michigan at his winter home in Palm Springs. After one lunch he hosted, I shared an update for the attendees, and when I asked if there were any questions, many shouted them out from around the room. President Ford raised his hand, while sitting in the center of the front row. I remember thinking to myself, if ever a person earned the right to speak up and take the floor, it was a former president. But that is not what he did. I was honored to acknowledge him and let him ask his very thoughtful and considerate question.

Later that afternoon, after golf, I asked President Ford if he would take a picture with my dad, my brother, and me, to which he replied, "I would be honored."

Here we are, with President Ford wearing a name tag! He had printed the name tag himself, and it said "Jerry Ford"— not "President Ford" or "Gerald Ford." He was just one of us.

Curiosity, with a Desire to Learn and Grow

Even the most intelligent person on earth cannot list what they do not know. Exceptional leaders are curious about why others think differently than they do. What insights can be gained by asking questions? They believe their growth and the team's growth are linked. And that very often, growth occurs when the leader is humble enough to cede problem-solving to the team. With humility and vulnerability, the leader can accept that they do not have all the answers. When problems arise, the opportunity for the best solutions—for the most growth—will come when the most diverse views are respected. The shift from leadership control over decision-making to shared decision-making is the shift from *me* to *team*.

> *From the CEO of a manufacturing company:*
>
> *"The biggest mistake you can make is to think you're smarter than the people who work for you. That's the beginning of the end for leaders. If I can get all their brains engaged and get the emotional stuff behind us, we all get better."*

As a leader, ask yourself:

- How curious are you about others who disagree or do not perceive things as you do?
- Are you open to the idea that your team's growth is linked to your growth?
- Do you have a picture of what your team looks like when performing at its peak?
- Do you believe you can make that Peak Performance Culture a reality?
- Are you open to the idea that your team can own the journey to Peak Performance with your coaching?

Exceptional leaders are constantly evolving and developing. As they work to grow themselves, they create a learning organization to stay relevant and effective, providing sustainability far into the future.

Are you open to the idea that your team can own the journey to Peak Performance with your coaching?

A Passion to Serve Others

When you have a passion to serve others, you care about how you make them feel and your impact on their lives. When team members get a hint that you are in it for yourself, you no longer have a loyal team that will go the extra mile.

From a university medical department chair:

"Sometimes people think they want to be a leader because then they have more power and more prestige. Those who do it for that reason tend to be less successful than those who do it because they say, 'Hey I've got some skills, I think I could be good at developing people, and I'm okay with getting my satisfaction from other people doing well rather than my own self doing well.' When you get to a point you understand that to be a successful leader, it's not about you. It's about people you are developing. You must be okay with getting your job satisfaction through your faculty member flourishing, rather than focusing on what accolades you can get."

We are all immature in the early stages of life, focused on a "me first" mindset. Even as mature adults our egos get in the way of what may be best for the team. While we never lose our egos, with maturity, we experience more meaningful and profound joy from helping others live thriving, valued, and meaningful lives.

Great leaders benefit others as they:

- reach down in the organization to positively impact others;
- help others on their journey to thrive with safer and more secure lives;
- understand that each of us is insecure and has doubts about our capabilities and potential;
- see more in others than others see in themselves;
- appropriately and individually challenge themselves and others to close the gap between where they are and where they desire to be;
- articulate a shared a compelling Vision;
- build the confidence of others by recognizing and celebrating their strengths;
- support others on their journey to living a life of meaning;
- recognize there is social responsibility in how they win.

The outdoor clothing and gear company Patagonia has redirected its Purpose and Vision from sales to supporting the sustainability of our planet. To improve their impact on future generations, they are committed to reducing the number of their products that eventually wind up in a landfill. They state:

> It's time for us as a company to address the issue of consumerism and do it head-on. The most challenging and meaningful element of the Common Threads Initiative is this: to lighten our environmental footprint. Everyone needs to consume less, and businesses need to make fewer things but of higher quality. Customers need to think twice before they buy.

Patagonia understands there is often a higher cost to being socially conscious, to caring about the impact we are having on others, so this impacts the prices they charge. They appeal to customers like me and many others who enjoy spending a little more to buy a quality product from a company that seeks to create a more sustainable planet for our grandchildren. They demonstrate integrity and build trust in their alignment to their Vision. We know their products are being made in the long-term best interest of all.

Exceptional leaders live purposefully at Stage III Fulfillment (Benefiting Others). Their efforts become sustainable with the following two attributes.

Authenticity (Building Trust with Actions)

Team members can sense if a leader can be trusted. Authentic leaders build trust. They share what they know, and they are open about what they don't know. They are there for the team, not for themselves. Sure, they have egos, but they understand their ego is only to be used in service of helping the team become better.

How often have we heard that our actions speak louder than our words? The actions of leaders are studied and focused upon like no other group of people. Exceptional leaders understand they are always under a microscope—there are no days off. It takes time to build trust, but it can be lost with one mistake. And it can take years to rebuild trust, if that is possible at all.

Dr. Judith Glaser, an organizational anthropologist and author of *Conversational Intelligence*, asserts that a great relationship is built on positive, respectful, and responsible communication that builds trust. Responsible and trust-building communication followed by appropriate action produces oxytocin and serotonin, which give the team the feeling of safety and security to think creatively, openly, and productively. This enhances the flow leaders are seeking.

Again, with humility, we can let ourselves be more purposefully vulnerable and, in turn, more trusted. This trust and the feeling of security it engenders is critical to the shift from *me* to *team* and the organization's long-term sustainability.

Deep Caring for Team Members

The desire of team members to be cared about is inherent and can be tapped into by leaders in many ways. Exceptional leaders understand the many facets of genuine caring, and they adjust and adapt as required to connect with their team individually and collectively.

Being cared for or cared about releases good hormones that let our body know we are safe; we feel that someone has our best interests at heart. We are more effective in this state, and our brain and muscles work better. When we are cared for and respected, we feel valued for our perspective and experiences, for being who we are.

Furthermore, we experience the feelings caused by these good hormones when caring for others. Acts of kindness can promote a circular system of caring at work, reinforcing the value of caring and creating a culture of safety and security. In this context, safety and security enable creativity and innovation to flourish.

We regularly experience the power of being cared about and respected at our full-day Culture Clarification retreats. One example surfaced with a manufacturing client. A team member who was around thirty years old shared a story about a mistake he made when he was a recent high school graduate and full-time employee of the company. He made a wrong decision and got into an accident that totaled his car. He was OK and had no injuries, but he had no car to get to work and no money to buy one.

With tears in his eyes, the man spoke of how company leadership believed in him and did not fire him. Instead, they invested in him by lending him money to buy a car and guiding him in becoming who he is today. Leadership continued to support him, and he repaid the loan paycheck by paycheck. Leadership mentored him in responsible decision-making, and, to this day, he is forever grateful. Even though he was immature, he was cared about and respected. He was believed in for who he was and who he could become. Today he is a vital employee mentoring others on their journey to greater maturity and responsibility.

From the leader of a healthcare not-for-profit:

"I wanted to be a CEO at age thirty-two. Yet, I became a CEO at fifty-eight and never imagined the personal work needed to become a good leader! We were doing alright before, but this work has put us in a much better place.

"My team looked at me as a hard worker. But they shared that I was a drive-by leader, meaning I was too busy doing the work to care about my team. Now that I know them personally, I care about each one at a completely different level. I'm still a long way from becoming the person I can be, but my progress has made a big difference in how our organization operates.

"I told my staff my 'why' at a staff meeting. It made me dig deep and say, 'Why do I care so much about this work? Why is this work so important to me?' I was able to open up. It was hard for me to be a leader and be open. That was a significant change for somebody like me—to be open and to be vulnerable.

"If you want people to grow themselves, you must share your growth, and you must keep growing. And that's not always easy. And for somebody like me, being vulnerable wasn't and still isn't easy for me, but it has made all the difference in who we have become."

Leaders show they care in small ways. They:

- humbly engage their team members in meaningful conversation for the team members' benefit;
- notice when a team member is struggling and offer help;
- recognize exceptional performances and offer support when team members struggle;
- humbly give support generously, not expecting anything in return.

Leaders show they care in more profound ways as well. They demonstrate deep caring. The following examples come from team members at a retreat in response to the request for stories of the organization when it was at its best.

- *One of our team members was diagnosed with cancer last year. She chose to follow a non-traditional method. We have held fundraisers to help her pay for everything insurance didn't cover.*

- *Our owner took time for a customer who could barely come up with the deposit for a $10,000 purchase while a much larger and more significant customer waited.*

- *We sponsor Christmas for an underprivileged school. T-shirts, breakfast and lunch, gifts, and, for some, family gifts; forty team members participated. And we end up feeling like the beneficiaries.*

- *I was young and stupid and got into trouble, and leadership at this company helped me get through the tough times. I would be in real trouble today if it were not for this company.*

Caring Goes Both Ways

In many cases, team members expect to be cared for but may not feel responsible for reciprocating and caring about the organization. Team members and leaders must remember Guiding Principles exist to serve the Purpose of the organization and apply to all. Team members are to ensure the organization's long-term sustainability if they want the organization to survive.

For example, during the worst of the COVID-19 pandemic, many workers got used to working from home as a requirement. As restrictions were lifted, some asked to continue their work from home. This may be fine for some organizations, but not for others. If working from home inhibits the organization from Peak Performance, then the Guiding Principle of caring is not being honored by the team member who wants to work from home. That is a demonstration of not caring about the organization that is providing the sustainability to create safety and security for all for the long term.

Deep caring needs to go two ways. The organization—via its leadership—cares for the team member, and the team member cares for the organization. Leadership needs to work with team members to establish how caring is defined within the organization. This includes explicitly stating that honoring what is best for the organization provides the safety and security most team members are seeking.

Clients who have clarified their Core Identity find elevated organizational decision-making taking place. We have found when four or more teammates openly discuss an issue, there is greater depth and understanding in the decision for the long term, rather than short-term self-interest. The shift from *me* to *team* becomes natural and is consistent with the human instinct to create a safer, more secure tomorrow for each other.

In our experience with clients, once there is clarity about the Core Identity, a group of four or more consistently makes decisions for a safer and more secure tomorrow for the organization.

While there are many attributes of great leadership, we have found the four outlined above—curiosity, a passion to serve others, authenticity, and deep caring—to be the fundamental requirements. It is about how we make others feel. Are we positively energizing our team in service of something much bigger than any of us could achieve alone? Are we consciously bringing new energy into the organization and encouraging others to do the same?

Leadership is a never-ending growth opportunity for those who love to learn and grow. New challenges develop daily, but leaders with these fundamental attributes enable their organization to solve problems and implement systems for sustainable success.

Leadership and Listening

Truly Listening to Survey Results

Leaders who have the attribute of curiosity, who desire to learn and grow, are open to feedback and curious about the perspectives revealed in survey results. With these leaders, respondents do not need to fear retribution for sharing their feelings and perspectives. Sharing is one thing, but engaging in open and honest discussions regarding the organization's current state requires all four leadership attributes described above. Listening to the results means being open to what the team members think and feel about the organization. It means the perspective of the person giving the feedback is to be respected. How their perspective is appreciated and respected impacts their feelings, and their feelings count; they are valid. Genuinely listening to and respecting the survey results—trusting in the process, caring about team members' lives—begins to set the stage for the subsequent growth that is to come.

From the CEO of a branding agency:

"I liked the idea of how FS/A would interview our team. The interviews were eye-opening and helped me on this journey. It helped me understand how people feel about the organization and the leadership. You think about things from your perspective as a leader. You think you have a handle on things. You think you know the people in your organization. When FS/A does these interviews, you realize pockets in your organization do not think as you thought, and we need to know that."

In preparing leadership for the retreat, we create a new relationship between the leader and the team. The shift from *me* to *team* will be manifested in the leader's new role at the retreat. We inform the leader that their job at the retreat is merely *to listen*. They may ask clarifying questions if they feel an erroneous statement is being made, but their primary focus will be on listening. By listening, they respect the perspectives of their team members, not just those of leadership. It's not about *displaying* trust. It's about *genuinely respecting* the process and the results. It's about *genuinely trusting* in the team's untapped greatness: the team's depth and diversity of knowledge, its vast and diverse experiences and perspectives, its desire to be exceptional. We have learned that human beings want to be a part of making a significant difference that benefits many. Leadership must trust that when it comes time to make decisions, big or small, by thoroughly engaging team members they unleash their collective greatness to render the best results for the team.

> *From a university medical department chair:*
>
> *"We are surgeons, and we are used to making decisions by ourselves and getting credit for our success. The FS/A culture process has taught us to think of others more and think in our team's best interest for the benefit of our patients.*
>
> *"I was surprised at the impact of giving power to the team. Instead of saying, 'Here's the solution,' we let the team develop a solution. It's like a magical thing. It works much better than me telling them, even if it is the same solution, and sometimes it's a better solution than mine."*

Listening means putting team members' lives and the organization's future ahead of the leader's desire for control. Authentic leadership is not about control or power; it's about engaging, energizing, and enabling team members to apply the greatness resident in them for sustainable organizational success.

Revealing Your Core Identity

The Retreat: Expectations

We start by asking: *To get the most out of this day together, how do we need to conduct ourselves?*

They come up with things like *openness, listening, honesty, respect, vulnerability,* etc. You can feel the atmosphere begin to change. It's not just about how they want this retreat to go; they're starting to talk about how they want to work together from this day forward.

The 20/60/20 Natural Fit Ratio Surfaces

During the several-months-long Culture Clarification process, most often we find that 20% of the team members in the organization are fully aligned, modeling and honoring the organization at its best. It is natural for them. Meanwhile, there seem to be about 20% who have little or no interest in what is best for the organization. They have their own best way of working. It is about them, not the team. They are self-focused, and they care only about what the organization can do for them. It has become clear that our work is to engage the 60% in the middle. It can be easy and natural for the 60% to adopt the Peak Performance culture, but they will need the organization's Reinforcing Systems to provide support to align actions and behaviors.

During the full-day retreat, when great stories of what the organization has looked like at Peak Performance are shared, the aligned 20% are engaged, but so are the middle 60% that are not as naturally aligned yet. The sizeable middle group is energized to see what could be. They know they have been there in the past, and they can get on board with Peak Performance becoming the standard.

With the proper Reinforcing Systems to help create new habits, the middle 60% are naturally and genuinely energized by the clarified alignment. At the same time, the 20% who are in it for themselves realize their lives are about to change.

Natural Fit Ratio

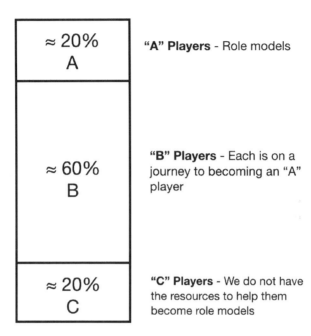

≈ 20%
A

"A" Players - Role models

≈ 60%
B

"B" Players - Each is on a
journey to becoming an "A"
player

≈ 20%
C

"C" Players - We do not have
the resources to help them
become role models

As Adam Grant shared in his book *Give and Take*, the energy drain in an organization from a "C" player (from your bottom 20%) requires the energy of three "A" players (from your top 20%) to counterbalance the drain.

Once the organization has a shared Core Identity, each team member can debate their concept of what it means, but it is no longer just their perspective that counts; the Core Identity belongs to the team—What is the team's perspective?

When "C" players play the game out of bounds, confusion over what is acceptable and not acceptable for Peak Performance surfaces, de-energizing and distracting the team. Leaders seldom understand the de-energizing impact and cost of out-of-bounds behaviors.

In Chapter 4, we will share Reinforcing Systems and the process of addressing team members who do not choose to grow and move toward Organizational Culture Fit.

The Key Role of Storytelling

Storytelling plays a significant role in Culture Clarification. Before the written word, all knowledge was passed through storytelling. Human beings are wired to learn and grow from storytelling. Stories paint pictures that lead to feelings that impact our decision-making. Stories connect to feelings of right and wrong, good and bad. Our values filter helps us stay on course, and it becomes stronger with tried-and-true stories of decision-making that led to the results we desired.

During the retreat, team members share stories of people doing their best under pressure, living up to their values/principles. These stories surface what we'd like to be more like as an organization. Themes that touch our feelings are the keys to the storytelling process. Team members experience the release of serotonin and oxytocin and are left feeling safer and more secure as a result.

Sharing stories of organizational Peak Performance, of people performing their best under pressure, has the power to change the lens through which team members view the organization and set expectations for themselves and each other. The purpose is to move the organization toward its strengths and capabilities.

As stories of significance surface, team members are emotionally moved. They are energized and grateful to have the opportunity to shape the organization's Core Identity. The retreat establishes storytelling as a means for team members to clarify what they look like at their best for today, setting the stage for actions tomorrow. **The goal is to convert the words that compose their carefully created Core Identity into feelings.** This takes time, but after the exemplary stories have been told for years, the words become feelings, aiding team members in reacting under pressure, more naturally, and at their best. This is the engine that drives the sustainability of the organization.

Revealing the Organization's Guiding Principles

Guiding Principles define how we like to be treated and how we like to treat others. Team members have a strong understanding of their feelings at work. To get the Culture Clarification process started, we begin with Guiding Principles.

Guiding Principles: *How teammates desire to work together for Peak Performance.* We share the many Guiding Principles revealed in the survey and ask team members to come prepared to lobby with exemplary stories for the three they feel must reside as a part of their Core Identity moving forward.

The Prompt: *Think about a story you would tell a significant other or a new employee that would paint a clear picture of the organization honoring this Guiding Principle at its best under pressure.*

Team members share stories in small groups and then share their best stories with the larger group. The energy is easy to feel. People are engaged in meaningful storytelling. We often hear stories about management and team members going above and beyond to help each other in a time of need. Management is listening to team members' perspectives. Team members engage each other in stories of "at our best." The energy in the room is genuine and heartfelt. People will remember this day when management asked them to share what was most meaningful to them and permitted them to set the standard for the organization's future.

From a university medical department chair:

"There were maybe sixty or seventy of us, and the team came up with the Guiding Principles, Purpose, and Vision. What they came up with felt right to me, but it came out of their mouths."

From the CEO of a brand-building agency:

"This has freed up energy—energy coming from the freedom of not dealing with problems that occupied so much of my time before we had employees invested in the values . . . who take ownership over keeping their work within the scope and realm of our values."

Who We Are Is in How We Treat Each Other

One of the mechanics who repaired large vehicles for a client shared with us, *"I was stuck underneath this truck with the wrong tool, and my hand was holding a part I could not let go. I thought I would have to put all this back together, crawl out, and try to find the tool I needed when one of my fellow mechanics bent over and asked me if I needed a hand. I asked him if he knew where the special tool could be found and could he retrieve it for me, a special tool others hid for their personal use. He was back with just the tool I needed in no time, and I could complete my project. This would not have happened at my previous employer. At this company, people have your back, and it's reassuring to know that when you're in a jam, somebody will be there for you."*

Allowing Feelings to Be Expressed

We focus on the positive picture we desire to create at the retreat. However, some team members have been hurt or upset by past events. They feel their values have been betrayed. It's like they carry a trash bag to collect all the wrongs committed against them over time. If they do not have the opportunity to dump the bag, the trash keeps building up. Through experience, we've learned that those who've been hurt cannot get past perceived violations until they have been respectfully heard. They *must* dump their bag of trash before they can move on.

Most often, these dumping events happen in our one-on-one interviews. However, they can surface during the retreat, and the emotion in dumping the wrongs is real, as is the respect they are given for their feelings. This creates trust in the process. Sometimes the trust created is so deep that those perceived to be the most negative end up being surprisingly engaged and supportive of the process moving forward.

Team members leave the retreat with a new awareness of how they are treating each other, what is good for the team, and what hurts the team's performance. We see the shifting from *me* to *team* taking place.

Revealing the Organization's Shared Purpose

The organization's Purpose is its *Why*. Why are we doing today's work?

Purpose: *That which brings meaning to life; the deep, non-financial reasons that get you out of bed in the morning energized to do your day's work.*

The stories team members share begin to show a much larger Purpose, a Purpose with a profound meaning—it is bigger than goals, profits, or prestige. The Purpose revealed in the Culture Clarification process is, inevitably, a desire to create shared success, to work in a way that benefits all stakeholders—team members, patients, customers, vendors, and the community.

Purpose Examples from Clients

Again, it is the emotional stories honoring your Purpose people will remember and bring context to the words below.

- *To provide a meaningful environment where our people can provide the highest-value service.*

- *Improve lives through curing, preventing, and treating eye disease.*

- *Developing and delivering care of the highest quality to improve lives today and tomorrow.*

- *To be a community that inspires greatness in each other.*

Revealing the Organization's Compelling Shared Vision

Our Purpose energizes us to get up and do our work today. Consider the Purpose examples above. Imagine a group of people working in service of their Purpose for years. Imagine the possibilities of generations working toward that purpose. What might that work make possible?

Vision: *The compelling image of the desired future we strive to make real in honoring our Purpose. We may never get there, but it is a guide for all strategic decision-making.*

Once team members have a clear, deeply meaningful Purpose, we challenge them to envision what their Purpose could make possible. It is common to have a short-term orientation due to the challenges of accomplishing tasks on the list today; it is difficult for us to think about the future. This exercise requires shifting to thinking decades or generations into the future. With patience and guidance, the team does get there.

Vision Examples from Clients

Again, it is the emotional picture of the tomorrow you hope to create with your Vision people will remember and brings context to the words below.

- *Confident and unrestricted lives through renewed health*

- *A company that respects and honors its heritage to enhance lives and create thriving communities for the next 100 years*

- *Our community is living lives of meaning through transformative eyecare.*

- *Healthy communities where all people achieve their most remarkable quality of life*

Individual Identities Meld into a Shared Core Identity

Each team member expresses what is best for the organization from their personal Core Identity perspective—their set of Guiding Principles, their Purpose, and their Vision. In the Culture Clarification process, the organizational Core Identity that emerges is a melding of these individual Core Identities. The like-minded majority create a shared energy that can be felt in the room as a state of flow develops from the clarified Core Identity.

While it seems that the Core Identity is being clarified, the reality is that the brand/culture/identity that attracted these people in the first place is now surfacing and becoming clearer. In reality, their *fit filter* was most likely active when they chose to join this organization, so this Core Identity is not by chance.

Whether individually or organizationally, honoring our Core Identity is a challenging process. We ask ourselves questions: *Why we are doing what we do? How do we like to be treated? How do we want to treat others?* We do this to be our best for something greater than ourselves.

Individually and organizationally, Core Identity clarification is a never-ending process. Life gets better with greater clarity and understanding over time. The twists and turns of our journey will continue. Now, we have a template for individual and organizational decision-making.

Honoring Your Core Identity

Essential Success Factors

Each team member has cast their vote. The organization's Purpose, Vision, and Guiding Principles have been drafted. We have the words, stories, and emotions of what the team looks and feels like when at Peak Performance.

What happens next?

Thousands of organizations have undertaken some version of Culture Clarification—writing mission, purpose, operating statements, etc.—without impacting the organization's daily operations and decision-making.

> **Honoring the Core Identity as the organization's compass means reinforcing the Core Identity . . . every day.**

How will team members honor the Core Identity moving forward? How do those Guiding Principles transition from words to an *internalized and systematized way of working together? How do we establish better habits?*

The question we pose to team members: *Imagine the success and sense of flow created because the Core Identity is honored. What are the requirements of the organization to change to make that possible?*

The following are examples of Essential Success Factors clients regularly share:

- Leadership role models the clarified culture.
- We are tweaking/adjusting current systems to honor our Core Identity better.
- We proactively and respectfully address violations of the Core Identity.
- We take time to share stories honoring our Core Identity.
- We celebrate exemplary behavior.
- We proactively seek feedback from stakeholders (patients, customers, vendors, community members, etc.) regarding their perception of who we are.
- We reference our Core Identity when tough decisions are made.

- We strategically plan with our Vision as the compass.
- All those being promoted honor our Core Identity.

Critical Failure Factors

In revealing the organization's Core Identity, team members are imagining an energizing culture. What could get in the way of that thriving state of flow?

The question we pose to team members: *What could derail the success of this culture that permits us to perform at our best? How might we fail to capitalize on the work we have done?*

The following are examples of Critical Failure Factors we regularly hear from clients:

- We do our work tomorrow the same way we did it yesterday.
- We do not call each other on confusing actions that seem to hinder "at our best" performance.
- Leadership does not try to role model "at our best."
- We do not take the time to celebrate "at our best" behaviors and decisions.
- We do not address the issue of individuals who seem to be self-interested at our expense.

Choosing Success or Failure

The desired culture embodied in the words of the Core Identity represents what the organization desires to be. But at this point, they are just words on a page. It's aspirational. The work to have the Core Identity of *who we are* is just beginning. Discussing the Essential Success Factors and Critical Failure Factors is a critical step toward identifying and implementing systems that will reinforce the Core Identity for the future.

A Client's Creative Representation of Core Identity

Integrity
The integrity of our office is based on honesty, respect, and trust.

Team
We are a unified team built on respect, communication, and fun.

Purpose
To make a difference in people's lives by improving their self-esteem.

Innovation
Our courage to innovate keeps us on the cutting edge.

Relationships
We build caring relationships through open communication, trust, compassion, and respect.

Excellence
We strive for excellence.

Vision
We will continually raise the standard of care through inspiration, motivation, and education.

A New "At Our Best"

The Retreat Experience

By the end of the Culture Clarification retreat, we experience two outcomes. The first outcome is an idea: it's a new "at our best" embodied in components of the clarified Core Identity and clarity about what Peak Performance looks and feels like.

The other outcome is a collection of tangible feelings based on the stories of the organization at its best from the retreat experience. For many, their engagement at work changes as the retreat demonstrates the leader as a listener. The leader demonstrates and models respect, trust, and curiosity by listening to team members tell stories, share feelings, take risks, and overcome vulnerability.

Team members come to see the leader as someone who values their stories, feelings, and ideas and respects their collective ability to make decisions that will shape the organization's future. They see themselves as capable and responsible, and they are invested in contributing to decision-making. They feel responsible for speaking up, even in situations when they previously may have been hesitant. The result is a sense of security in sharing thoughts and opinions. They feel the shift from *me* to *team* as decision-making has been transferred from individual responsibility to collective responsibility. They feel that growth and change are possible. They are energized that this is the organization's most effective path forward.

Collectively, those feelings may be described as *hope*—hope that the organization's shift from *me* to *team* will continue.

As a leader, how will you honor and respect that hope?

Doing your part in helping align the organization to its Core Identity will build the trust, respect, and caring the team has for you. It means you will realize the responsibility of leadership to fulfill your role to ensure the journey to unleashing organizational greatness continues.

Letting hope die will erode trust and can be devastating to your organization. We warn leaders: *Do not undertake this Culture Clarification process unless you are committed to following through to honor what your team creates. Your team has hopes they can become something special. This exercise illuminates that they can be special. Not executing to honor your clarified Core Identity tells your team, "We do not care about being exceptional, nor do we desire to seek Peak Performance." Soon your "A" players will leave for a more fertile garden.*

Ultimately, what happens after the retreat is up to leadership.

In the following chapter, we'll discuss Reinforcing Systems that will help honor the standard the team has set. Reinforcing Systems enable new, more purposeful habits to be created. They deepen the understanding of the Core Identity, clarify the boundaries of the Guiding Principles, and ensure that the energizing journey toward the organization's Vision is sustainable.

Questions to Consider

- Is leadership listening with trust, respect, and curiosity?
- Do team members feel safe expressing themselves?
- Are we remembering and telling exemplary stories that define us at our best?
- Do we believe team members are doing their best with what we have given them, and are we challenging them?

Chapter Takeaways

- The 20/60/20 Natural Fit Ratio breaks down as follows:
  - 20% of your team members will role model the organization at its best
  - 60% will follow the road of least resistance
  - 20% will challenge you on what is best for the organization

- Exceptional leaders possess the following attributes, with the common thread of humility:
  - curiosity, with a desire to learn and grow
  - a passion to serve others
  - authenticity (building trust with actions)
  - deep caring for team members
- Old habits die hard. Peak Performance requires new purposeful habits.
- Understand your Essential Success Factors and Critical Failure Factors.

CHAPTER 4

REINFORCING SUSTAINABLE SUCCESS

What happens in life is not as random as we may think. Most of life's successful and unsuccessful actions are reactions to forces already in place. Many of these forces are in our control and can be created strategically and purposefully for predictable and desired results.

Through the Culture Clarification process, the organization has revealed the Purpose, Vision, and Guiding Principles that compose its Core Identity at Peak Performance. This surfaces an intrinsic desire to succeed *together*. As team members realize what they can achieve together, they leave the retreat, and the shift from *me* to *team* has begun. The feeling of positive energy and a positive future is taking hold.

There are two requirements for successfully reinforcing the Peak Performance culture:

- systems and disciplines that institutionalize Peak Performance
- proactive leadership support of those systems and disciplines

Most—about 80%—will understand and agree with the alignment process, but a minority may perceive it as a major inconvenience. As you may have witnessed from experience, some team members want to work their way, regardless of the agreed upon standards, and can be disruptive. The Reinforcing Systems support the majority who desire to work together as one team, and they are encouraged, within the Guiding Principles, to proactively address issues with those who stray from the standards agreed upon.

Whom will they follow? The 20/60/20 alignment ratio referred to earlier will apply here. We have found that the top 20% come into the clarification process motivated by a strong sense of purpose, and they become more and more unified. With this common bond, they are committed to the organization's clarified vision of a better tomorrow.

We find that the retreat will energize the middle 60%. They like the clarity of where the organization is going; it resonates with them. However, they will need reinforcement and reminders to sustain the energy from the retreat and create new habits. The remaining 20% may create roadblocks to inhibit this shared way of thinking they do not support.

How mature is the team? The organization's Core Identity is anchored by a Purpose and Vision that will energize mature team members who value *team* and *community* success over *individual* success.

Those lacking in maturity—recall Stage II Fulfillment (Learning, Growing, and Competing)—may still be driven by their egos for personal achievement in the short term. A sustainable transformation depends on the systematic proactivity that reinforces organizational growth as they shift from *me* to *team*.

How do we change old habits? Habits developed over time become ingrained. Some habits have enabled the individual to succeed at the team's expense. The pull of old habits is strong, especially under pressure, but habits need to change to make the shift from *me* to *team*. We understand that respectful patience is a requirement when it comes to changing habits. It takes time, but eventually, there must be alignment to be a sustainable and peak-perfoming team.

Reinforcing Systems Support Peak Performance

Collegiate athletic teams first showed me the power of consistent boundaries. If players continued to run out of bounds, they didn't play. If they didn't go to class, they didn't play. If they showed up late, they didn't play. Because all wanted to play, they stayed in bounds. The exceptional coaches continually assessed the boundaries and alignment, even anticipating when boundaries may be stretched.

We refer to these purposeful, disciplined practices that reinforce the Core Identity as *Reinforcing Systems*.

In the business world, we have boundaries, but the ramifications for violating them seldom take the violator out of the game! Violators continue to get paid, and we have found that some are even rewarded for playing out of bounds.

After the retreat, the Core Identity initially exists as a set of meaningful words and ideas. To whatever extent the ideas energize members of the organization, there is a long way to go before they become intrinsic *feelings*.

From the CEO of a branding agency:

"As now we have principles and values to help us get where we're going, we can create systems to help us. And those systems are Reinforcing Systems. It wasn't FS/A telling us to do these exact things, it was them sparking us to think on our own about how to do this. Now we have electronic kudos boards so anything positive within the company gets recorded and tagged to a certain Value. Now it's not just a value, but it's a story of a Value in action. We have stand up meetings where we used to talk about work-work-work. Now we're talking about how we're feeling, how we're doing, who is doing well, who needs help. So, it's this different way of solving the same issues, but the effectiveness is much greater and impactful."

Caring is an essential Guiding Principle and surfaces in each organization. Despite a collective agreement that caring must be valued, each team member possesses their interpretation of what caring is to them.

How do we move from multiple interpretations of caring to a mutually shared understanding?

When Reinforcing Systems are put in place, acts of caring will be recognized and celebrated. This needs to be true each time the principle of caring is violated. As acts of caring are recognized, and stories that exemplify caring are told, the organization's idea of what it means to care moves from words to feelings. *"Does this feel right for the team?"* will permeate the organization as an aligning force. Through celebrating acts of caring and addressing violations, the boundaries become apparent. It becomes clear which actions fall *in bounds* and *out of bounds* of the Guiding Principle of caring for the organization.

The Effectiveness of Disciplined Reinforcing Systems

In this work, we have experienced transformational change that can be apparent in a few months. People adapt very quickly as honoring your Core Identity taps into the natural human desire to build a protective community. We intrinsically understand this is the way we are meant to work together. It feels right. However, old habits die hard, and it often takes longer for flow to occur. When the organization is dedicated to honoring its Peak Performance Culture and is disciplined in implementing Reinforcing Systems, this process has the power to enable the transformative change all can feel. And it can happen quickly.

A client in the medical device business with an exceptional product was led by two gifted leaders with a team of talented young people passionate about their business. They were in growth mode, hiring fast and growing even more quickly. Yet, leadership knew they were not performing at Peak Performance and asked for our help.

The challenge was that the two leaders, who were gifted salespeople, spent most of their time and energy externally, leaving a team of inexperienced team members to run daily operations. Understandably, the *me* mindset was present in the young team, yielding ineffective processes.

Within three months of clarifying their Peak Performance Core Identity and understanding what the organization looks like when at its best, a transformational change took place. The partners shared, *"When we hired you, we never dreamt we could achieve where we are today, that this state would ever be possible."*

Clarify the Boundaries

Guiding Principles may have been established, and everyone in the organization must understand what those principles mean. Each team member will have a feeling for what is in bounds and out of bounds.

They have been encouraged to celebrate behaviors that align with the shared Peak Performance Core Identity and address behaviors that don't, thus ensuring that organizational boundaries are respected.

There was an uproar during the medieval period when boundaries—a musical notation system—were put on music being created. There was significant demand for music throughout Europe, but it was passed on by imitating what was heard, and there could be many variations. The time was ripe for developing a written form of musical notation. Instead of the sporadic, listen/learn/play passing on of music to the next generation, standardizing the documentation would ensure consistency. Some feared the limited number of notes would restrict creativity. Would this boundary stifle growth and the creation of innovative music?

The fears evaporated after implementation of the musical notation system. The proliferation of music was unprecedented. Boundaries can, indeed, enhance creativity.

Reinforcing the Right Thing to Do—Coach Red Berenson

University of Michigan's legendary Ice Hockey Coach Red Berenson is one of those rare leaders blessed with an innate sense of how to build teams for sustainable success. Early one Friday morning when I was Associate Athletic Director, Red Berenson came into my office. He said, "I have a problem. Our premier player is not going to class, and we have a team commitment: You go to class, you play; you do not go to class, you do not play. We play Michigan State tonight and tomorrow, and whoever wins these games wins the conference championship. And it is Parents' Weekend, so if we lose, I will get a lot of heat."

Red was a master leader. I affirmed that he was the head coach; only he knew what was right for the team. Whatever he decided, the Athletic Department would support him.

Red benched the player, the most successful goalie in the history of the NCAA. He showed the players that this team is special; it is not for everyone. It requires a commitment to something bigger than yourself. Michigan State won the conference championship, but something happened to the Michigan team.

All on the team heard the message: There is a responsibility to be a member of this remarkable team. Our standards are meant for every team member, with no exceptions.

Luck has a hand in winning National Championships, but you must be hitting on all cylinders to stay in the hunt. Michigan lost the conference championship that year but went on to win the NCAA National Championship.

Did benching the premier player play a role in this team's success? Removing any confusion about the importance of upholding the team's standards enabled the team to stay focused on their challenges. There are no shortcuts to long-term success, and there can be no distractions.

Red Berenson understands how to build unified teams for sustainable success.

Coach Berenson's stand had a double impact. The team's identity was reinforced, resulting in the reward of a National Championship. And the player found someone who cared about him and his personal development. If he wanted to be a leader, there was a standard that had to apply to him; today he is an admired and respected leader himself. Two identities were strengthened through one counterintuitive leadership decision.

The Stage III Fulfillment (Benefiting Others) reinforcement by Red exemplifies the responsibility of leadership. The best leaders build teams with members who understand they represent something bigger than themselves. This contrasts with pursuing the short-term Stage II Fulfillment (Learning, Growing, and Competing) gratification of winning the conference championship.

Capitalizing on Your Foundation of Greatness

When there is a lack of organizational alignment, it is just a matter of time before a significant issue will need to be addressed. Clarifying what you look like at your best provides the opportunity for establishing in-bounds and out-of-bounds behaviors. And in turn, the opportunity to honor and address the boundaries for greater clarity moving forward. We have many examples, from a startup company removing one of five partners before beginning operation to another business ending a seventeen-year partnership.

The startup breakup was more manageable, as funding was in the early stages, and success was still a dream. The dissolution of the long-standing partnership was much harder. It began unwinding when it became clear that the challenges and problems in the office were the result of one of the partners not taking responsibility for modeling the expected behavior. The exemplary partner was apprehensive about leaving and did not want to break up what was working, as rough as the current operating practices might be.

It took the better part of a year for the exemplary partner to establish their practice. Not only did they survive, but they are flourishing as they never dreamt possible. The desire for their services continues to outpace their ability to meet the demand.

This was FS/A's first opportunity to prove that if you understand your Foundation of Greatness as described in the Introduction, and there is a market for your services, you will thrive. Just as each of us individually possess a Foundation of Greatness, each organization possesses a Foundation of Greatness. *The community benefits when leadership respects that there is a Foundation of Greatness that they possess for sustainable success.*

Aligning Habits for the Team

With a shared *team* culture, the organization's potential exponentially expands. But getting there is a journey of systematized reinforcement of their Core Identity. The result is a shared understanding of the Core Identity and how leadership and team members treat each other, and a feeling of safety and security necessary for the successful journey to the compelling Vision.

Reinforcing the Core Identity is supported by these practices:

- integrating telling stories of the organization "at our best" as a regular practice
- assessing team members, teams, and operational systems for alignment to the Core Identity
- sharing metrics of alignment to the Core Identity
- developing committees led by team members to institutionalize the culture (detailed later in the chapter)
- leadership addressing out-of-bounds behaviors
- leadership assisting those who do not make progress in aligning to the Core Identity with training, and eventually to find another garden for them to thrive
- leadership reinforcing the Core Identity via decision-making and dynamic planning

Who Are We Under Pressure?

When everything is running smoothly, it's easier for team members to demonstrate their shared best selves in honoring the organization's

Telling Our Story

Who are we when at our best?

Use the Power of Storytelling

Storytelling has been a defining feature of humanity since the beginning of time. Stories help us explain ourselves and understand others. The stories we tell about our organization—and that others tell about us—share our brand, our culture, our identity.

Share Stories of What You Look Like at Your Best

Create a reinforcing discipline in your organization: Start every meeting with one story of what the organization has looked like at its best recently.

As the team members share stories, identify key components of your identity, for example:
- What is your Purpose? Is it consistent with Stage III Fulfillment (Benefiting Others)?
- What are your Guiding Principles? Are they helping you perform at your best and move forward effectively?

This may start slowly, but it will build over time and become one of the most powerful tools you possess. It will help you make faster and better decisions as you move forward honoring what you look like when at your best. Your culture will begin synthesizing naturally around the pictures being created from the stories. You may be surprised by the commonality you find in the most energized stories from all levels of the organization. Over time, you will surface the Foundation of Greatness that you can formalize with words supported by many stories of what you look like when at your best.

Core Identity. However, we may revert to self-interested old habits when pressures come to bear (deadlines approaching, last-minute demands from management or clients, tech failures, home challenges, etc.). These bad habits can include playing it safe by withdrawing from needed confrontations, or by keeping quiet instead of speaking up when the culture is compromised.

Disciplined Reinforcing Systems support the alignment with the organization's Core Identity, so in time it becomes a natural habit under pressure. Reinforcing Systems support alignment and address violations of the Core Identity. With Reinforcing Systems in place, most team members appreciate the reminders, and as a result, they are now helping set the new standards. They *feel* the positive results reinforcing the creation of new, better habits. And they become energized to be a part of an organization that is creating a safe place to thrive—especially when under pressure.

The Peril of Reinforcing Bad Habits

Many organizations claim a team-oriented Purpose, but their Reinforcing Systems reward a *me* orientation and pit team members against each other. This confuses and frustrates team members, and it hampers their ability to fully engage in their work. Confusing and counterproductive Reinforcing Systems may include these features:

- competitive commission-based incentive programs
- valuing the talent of team members over Organizational Culture Fit
- hiring team members for talent or friendship, irrespective of Culture and Behavior Fit
- rank comparing of team members

Organizations with Reinforcing Systems misaligned with their Values see their team struggle. Team members come to see terms like *values*, *principles*, and *mission* as talking points, used by leadership when it's convenient and then ignored for expediency. Team members do not trust leaders who invoke culture this way. Feelings of safety and security erode, and team members opt to look out for themselves. They do not speak up when the organization seems to be going astray. And the organization's "A" players realize their garden is no longer fertile ground for them to thrive, and they leave.

Leaders Need to Listen to Dissenters

It is easy for leaders to look at dissenters and outliers as problems. With caring being a required Guiding Principle, leaders must be respectful enough to hear people out. Leadership can become distanced from daily operations and too focused on metrics. It is easy for leadership to forget that how the team operates together determines the metrics.

It is common for team members—even the introverted—with values deeply aligned to the organization's to be the canaries in the coal mine because *"they just can't take it anymore."* The confusion is too much! Leaders need to respect dissenters and hear them out, because they often delineate how the organization has strayed from its Core Identity. For their own safety, and the security of the organization, dissenters need to be able to voice their concerns. Then, leadership can determine whether there has been a miscommunication, or if the organization has strayed, or if the dissenter may not be a good fit for the organization.

In our Culture Clarification interviews, we tell team members their responses are confidential and there will be no attribution. Too often, we hear, "I do not care if they know my feelings, this place must get better, or they can fire me—something has to change!"

Often, these outliers keep an organization from going off track. Respect the dissenters because they may be saying exactly what leaders need to hear.

Fit—Alignment with the Core Identity

Organizational Culture Fit

We use the term *Fit* to describe alignment to the Core Identity (*Organizational Culture Fit*) and alignment to the *competencies* and *behaviors* required by a job (*Job Fit*).

Does a team member fit the organization's culture?

Is the team member committed to aligning with the Guiding Principles, Purpose, and Vision the team created?

As some team members shift from *me* to *team,* their unselfish transition helps other team members align with the organization's Core Identity. Team member Fit increases as the boundaries of the Core Identity are more clearly understood and honored. Their Fit grows as they become more purposeful with their every action. As they feel greater joy in team success over their own, the culture becomes more robust; there is an increasing sense of collective safety and security.

A leader may believe that considering *Fit* when recruiting new hires means bringing in people that look and think as they do. *Did the person go to the same university? Are they the same religion or political bent? Do they speak the same language? Will the new hire fit in with the group that socializes after work? Do they look like me? Do they act like me?*

But those are not ingredients of Organizational Culture Fit. Organizational Culture Fit means aligning with the organization's Peak Performance Core Identity—its Purpose, Vision, and Guiding Principles—and that is all.

The Power of Diversity

Studies looking at complex problem-solving show that the best results are achieved when the deciding members represent significant diversity—a broad range of perspectives honoring your Core Identity. The key to the most effective outcomes in problem-solving and decision-making is to ensure that the group charged with coming up with the solution:

- possesses the rudimentary competency to contribute to the solution
- possesses as much diversity of perspectives as possible

while

- being committed to honoring the organization's Peak Performance Core Identity

From a university medical department chair:

"Everyone has a slightly different perspective. People have made suggestions that have worked out great. One of the things I talked about is diversity, specifically gender diversity. There are not a lot of women in leadership in this area. You're stronger if you have a diverse team because everyone has a slightly different perspective. One of my vice-chairs might say to me, 'Oh, I think we should do things this way,' and maybe I thought we should do it another way, but once I think about it, their solution is better than mine. You must engender that feeling of trust and respect that someone can give their ideas without worrying that they'll be made fun of, upset someone, or face retribution."

What Is Made Possible When Caring Is Reinforced?

- A shared understanding of what caring means within the organization, what behaviors fall within the boundaries (in bounds), and which do not (out of bounds);
- Feelings of safety and security that come from knowing all are on the same page;

- A growth in team members' trust that caring is not merely given lip service in the organization;

- Teammates who internalize and take responsibility for their caring about others and the organization as much as themselves;

- A feeling that caring is contributing to the journey toward realizing the compelling Vision;

- The creation of a community of caring team members that is creating a safe place to work;

- A feeling among clients and customers—everyone who interacts with the organization—that the organization cares about each of them.

Committees Can Institutionalize Your Culture

When we end the Culture Clarification retreat, we ask team members to identify Essential Success Factors and Critical Failure Factors to ensure the Core Identity becomes the organization's compass. What will guarantee success in aligning the organization to its Core Identity? What can prevent this effort from succeeding?

Our clients create several committees to assess where they are, where they need to be, and how to implement required adjustments to better align with the Core Identity. Clients have consistently and successfully formed committees to institutionalize their Core Identity. They generally create four to six committees. Some committees are the same across organizations. For example, most organizations have recognition programs to highlight exemplary performance by team members. The Rewards and Recognition Committee's initial job is to realign how and why it recognizes excellence. Team members will now be acknowledged and recognized for exemplifying the organization's Core Identity—its Purpose, Vision, and Guiding Principles—which is vital to developing new habits. They will not be recognized for anything else. No action should be recognized if it is not in alignment with the Peak Performance Culture.

From the CEO of a manufacturing company:

"We created committees—culture, hiring, and awards—for what I used to take responsibility for. Now, they're automatic; there's a system in place when someone gets hired/onboarded. We meet with them to see how they are doing from time to time. If they're not fitting with what we're trying to accomplish, we act quickly to help them or get them out. Before, we used to let people linger because they're good at X part of their job, so they'll figure the rest out. That is when we find ourselves in a gray area no one likes. Because of the systems, everyone knows what we're trying to accomplish. Confusion is addressed quickly."

The work of the Core Identity committees is distributed to team members representing diverse parts of the organization. Leadership asks for volunteers. We encourage identifying emerging leaders—even those who may not see themselves as leaders or may not have a conventional leadership background—but are passionate about what the organization can become. Most are honored when asked to participate, and they take their responsibility seriously.

The impact of these committees cannot be underestimated. These committees become influencers that penetrate every aspect of the organization. The natural desire to work together becomes a force needed to address the doubters, who surface and do not want to see this culture realized. These committees are one of the most impactful initiatives you can implement for creating a sustainable movement toward achieving your Peak Performance Culture.

From a university medical department chair:

"We definitely use our Guiding Principles in hiring. We have a Hiring and Retention Committee, and they've come up with a series of questions to assess someone's Culture Fit in our institution relative to the Guiding Principles. Occasionally we make mistakes. You hire someone and they're not quite the fit you thought they were going to be. But we haven't made any big mistakes. You invest a lot of money up front, and if they don't work out and they leave, you've invested the money without getting anything back."

Again, each organization will create its committees based on their response to the Essential Success Factors and Critical Failure Factors to ensure successful culture adoption. Each organization is unique and understands what committees are needed to reinforce the clarified Core Identity properly. The following are examples of standard committees our clients have formed.

From the CEO of a branding agency:

"I had been in charge of all personnel transactions. I was in charge of those relationships, in charge of what was in-bounds and out-of-bounds. I spent a lot of time trying to deal with people and issues. Because the team became the writer of the rules, and therefore the enforcer of the rules, I can step back and watch, and step in only when it's truly necessary. It's become self-monitoring. Because the team came up with it, they are empowered to make sure that we all are in-bounds. We've created the company DNA; it takes care of itself."

Committee Development

Organizational Core Identity Implementation
Who are we when at our best?

The committees will address these questions, based upon the clarified Vision, Purpose, and Guiding Principles for your organization:

1. What **objective key metrics** would provide an organizational dashboard on success?

2. What **critical success factors** would ensure the desired culture is honored?

3. What **critical failure factors** could undermine honoring the desired culture?

Suggested committees composed of diverse members of the organization

Culture Committee	**Roll Out Committee**
Fosters organizational culture alignment	Designs kickoff celebration of clarified Core Identity
Rewards and Recognition Committee	**Communications Committee**
Aligns rewards with Core Identity	Communicates about the clarified Core Identity
Hiring and Retention Committee	**Disciplined Strategic Planning Committee**
Ensures Culture Fit	Ensures progress towards Vision

Committees Set Bottom-up Disciplines

- Committees reinforce the shift from *me* to *team*, integrating the Core Identity into every aspect of the organization's operations.

- The committees reinforce the shift from *me* to *team* by putting decision-making into the hands of groups of team members from any level of the organization. The responsibility for the organizational alignment is shifted from leadership to the entire team.

- The committees reinforce the use of powerful storytelling to connect "doing" to "feeling" at its best.

- Their work reinforces a positive mindset, celebrating successes that set them up for more successes.

- Every committee reinforces the Core Identity by ensuring continual growth aligned to the Purpose, Vision, and Guiding Principles as their only goal.

- While Committee members work to reinforce the organization's Core Identity, perhaps more importantly, they are also internalizing personal alignment in their hearts and minds.

The Enablers of Peak Performance

> In looking for someone to hire, you look for three qualities: integrity (culture fit), intelligence (competency fit), and energy (behavior fit). But the most important is integrity because if they don't have that, the other two qualities—intelligence and energy—are going to kill you.
>
> —WARREN BUFFETT

Traditionally, Job Competency Fit has been the easiest and only Fit component assessed, whether in the hiring process or for performance reviews. Peak Performance requires the assessment of two other factors: Organizational Culture Fit and Job Behavior Fit. More than forty years of studying sustainably successful teams has revealed that Organizational Culture Fit is the most critical factor for sustainable Peak Performance. There is no substitute, and there are no shortcuts, thus this book's Organizational Culture Fit emphasis.

Peak Performance Equation for Individuals

| Peak Performance | = | Organizational Culture Fit | + | Job Competency Fit | + | Job Behavior Fit |

The Peak Performance Equation

This equation helps us create one evaluation form to be used in the hiring process, as well as the retention process.

Job Competency Fit is currently the focus of most performance reviews. It is objective. Assessing for Organizational Culture Fit is uncommon, as it is subjective and requires more time and thought. However, our clients rave about the increased return on investment gained when they take the time to assess Organizational Culture Fit. They are delighted by the significant difference in the fit of their new hires.

Organizational Culture Fit enables the flow required for sustainable Peak Performance. The team member is honoring the shared Core Identity, and there is a natural fit to align with its components:

- a compelling **Purpose**
- an inspiring **Vision**
- shared **Guiding Principles** (about five)

Culture assessment is subjective, but as an organization better understands the depth of storytelling, it can create an objective means to assess elements of the stories prospective hires tell, as well as decipher team members' feedback in performance reviews. In time, assessing alignment to the organization's Core Identity can be tied to specific components (Purpose, Vision, and Guiding Principles) for more objective decision-making on hiring and retention.

From a client CEO in the professional services industry:

"You bring in someone talented but maybe doesn't fit the culture, and it's like, perhaps they'll work out, maybe they'll fit in . . . but then you realize problems arise because you were not clear what kind of people belong; there was no clear distinction. Once you define who you are at your best, you recognize out-of-bounds, you don't allow violators to play, and you don't get in trouble.

"We have had five-star talent who all they wanted was self-promotion. I'd rather have three-star talent that wants to grow."

Job Competency Fit identifies the components the team member needs to do their job:

- **talent** - the gifts we are born with

- **skill** - the learned ability to do something well

- **knowledge** - the pertinent information needed to be effective

We have found that the best way to assess Job Competency Fit is to have objective metrics that demonstrate progress or achievement. Objective metrics leave little doubt about what success looks like. The team must understand that they must honor the Peak Performance Core Identity while seeking to achieve goals.

One of our clients shared, "Often, we are challenged with whom to hire. One has a strong Organizational Culture Fit but a weaker Job Competency Fit, while the other has a strong Job Competency Fit but a weaker Organizational Culture Fit. Which one should we hire?"

While Organizational Culture Fit is more challenging to assess than Job Competency, leaders find assessing becomes easier over time. And as they honor the organization's culture, it makes life better for all, and it enables a sustainably successful future.

That said, if Culture Fit is good, then the greater the Competency Fit, the faster the team member will realize success.

Job Behavior Fit illuminates how the team member makes others in the organization feel and includes these components:

- **passion** for their job within our business

- **positive energy**

- **appropriate behavior when under pressure for this job**

The Peak Performance Evaluation

These three factors of the Peak Performance Equation require deep understanding; as discussed above, each has components within it:

- Organizational Culture Fit - Purpose, Vision, and five Guiding Principles
- Job Competency Fit - talent, skill, and knowledge
- Job Behavior Fit - passion, positivity, and behavior under pressure

We have asked team members to create their Peak Performance evaluation form to measure these thirteen components of Peak Performance from the template in Appendix B. Adding a metric that identifies successful Peak Performance for each component aids in understanding what success looks like.

Ownership of their performance review is a generative process that improves as the team member better understands their job. The team member can participate in updating and improving their evaluation form to better assess their performance. In time, it clearly assesses what enables the organization to reach Peak Performance as each team member is learning and growing in their job.

From the CEO of a consumer products company:

"Before we worked with FS/A, performance reviews were about what you produced without regard to how you produced it. The reviews didn't consider how you treated people and those types of things. We now continue to assess performance, but the definition of Peak Performance Culture puts a premium on our values. We have people self-assess: Tell us how you're living up to this specific value. It's changed our perspective on evaluations from a 'must-do' to a 'want-to-do.' It's also changed what success looks like for our people. I like to get stuff done. But what I didn't realize until this work was the importance of how we get the work done. We were inside our heads, just charging ahead, without regard to the impact on others. But we were breaking apart because of personal relationship issues. FS/A has helped us connect the dots . . . our success is directly related to the energy we provide, and that has to do with how we treat each other. Our performance evaluations now enable us to create habits that reinforce who we are at our best."

Closing the Performance Gap

It is safe to say there will always be a gap or growth opportunity for a team member in one of the thirteen components of the Peak Performance Equation. Therefore, closing the Peak Performance gap is only possible when we reflect on the assessment, focusing on the component gaps to learn and grow to realize Peak Performance.

Each of us is on a personal Peak Performance journey to close the gap between where we are and need to be in our lives. The journey capitalizes on the successes and challenges that help us refine our actions and set a new standard for our own Peak Performance. Critically, the assessment results are the basis for the team member's game plan for improvement. We are on the move, on a continual growth journey toward our Vision of what we can become. Human nature continually challenges us to become who we are meant to be more fully. On this journey that never ends, we are getting better.

Be consistent and frequent in assessing and discussing initiatives to close the gap. We know it is human nature to be unhappy *when we do not know*. Assessments help people know. Do not be afraid to use them to let people know where they stand, but be there to support them and help them close their gaps. The industry trend is moving away from annual reviews to continual feedback on how we are growing; people do not like wondering how they are doing.

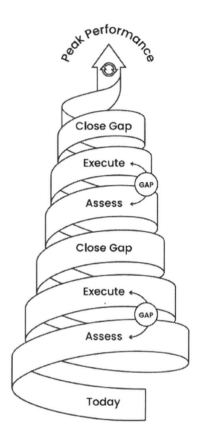

Peak Performance Growth Spiral

Assessing the Performance Gap

Humans are driven to strive for continuous improvement, but we first need to know where we are versus the Peak Performance standard for each of the thirteen performance assessment components. You have metrics to measure organizational success, and likewise, there can be metrics for team member effectiveness. However, we need to ensure team members are set up with effective systems for success.

Four areas should be assessed in this order:

1. Operating systems effectiveness
2. Individual team member effectiveness
3. Team effectiveness
4. Organizational effectiveness

Assess Operating Systems First

Often, we blame team members for poor performance when a deeper investigation reveals systems, rather than people, are not aligned with the Core Identity. Aligning operational systems to the Core Identity is the first step in improving team member morale and effectiveness. This demonstrates leadership's commitment to setting the team member up for success.

System Failure: Impossible Goal

For one client, the most significant stressor on team members was meeting month-end production goals. They pulled forward next month's production to meet this month's goals. The result was an intense production effort the last days of the month, and employees often had to work Saturdays and Sundays. This caused challenges at home, and the stress carried over to the plant. The shared short-term adrenaline rush, sacrifice, and success in accomplishment had become addictive. The team spent the first week of the following month patting each other on the back and recovering from the exceptional effort. The lack of production in the first week created a cycle that repeated month after month. It became clear that the adrenaline rush and pats on the back for achieving the impossible goal were profoundly satisfying and ingrained in the company's culture. The employees hated the stress and what it did to their family life, but they did not change their habits. They were addicted to the rush.

System Failure: Ineffective Inventory Tracking

We had a client who took out a significant loan to buy inventory because they wanted to ensure they did not run out, as they were unsure how much stock they had on hand. The antiquated inventory system inhibited them from being as effective as possible. They invested in a new inventory system and reduced their financial inventory commitment.

Assessing Team Members

A one-on-one interview with Coach Bo Schembechler was the final hurdle for a Michigan football recruit to determine if they would be offered a spot on the team. In this interview, Bo asked questions that revealed how well they would fit the team. He didn't use the term *organizational culture fit*, but that was what he was doing when he said he was assessing for "character."

It took years of study to understand what Bo was doing when deciding who would get an offer, those he would research more, and those who did not fit. One thing was clear: he prioritized Michigan's culture and its values of *integrity, caring for each other, growing, and the team* over talent. As a result, some High School All-Americans—some of the best players in the country—were not a fit for Michigan. And then there were much less skilled players who became captains of the Michigan team because of their character.

Leadership prioritizing Organizational Culture Fit is consistent with our research on sustainable Peak Performance. Once Culture Fit is in place, increased Competency Fit (talent, skill, and knowledge) and Job Behavior Fit (the ability to perform at a high level under pressure) enhances the journey to Peak Performance.

360° Assessments

To evaluate performance, we find that the best results come when team members receive multiple perspectives on their performance. We strongly recommend that 360° assessments, as this type of assessment is known, be implemented in every organization striving for Peak Performance.

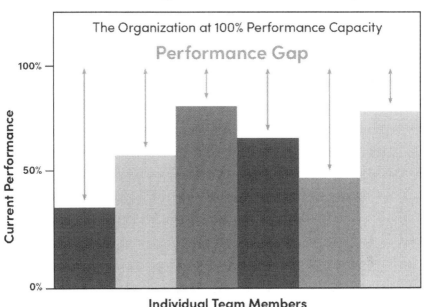

Before implementing 360° assessments, trust must be established for the assessment to be effective. Without trust, the data will not be respected, and the effort could backfire.

With the help of our clients, we have developed the assessment form in Appendix B referenced previously. This assessment can be used for all levels of the organization. This same form is used for annual reviews as well as in the hiring process.

The evaluators provide brief stories that support each component rating. For example, stories about the team member honoring the Core Identity go under Organizational Culture Fit. If possible, add an Objective Key Metric (OKM) for each story. In addition, each team member completes a self-assessment.

A complementary benefit of this process is that the individuals assessing—the contributing supervisor and team members—will almost assuredly wonder how others will be rating them on each component. This introspection and reflection reinforce the desired growth for the reviewer.

From an academic medical center chairperson:

"When I arrived, it was 'we do whatever we want, whenever we want.' There was no responsibility to anyone but themselves. The residents were treated poorly. The residency was on probation. It was not a good situation. So, we started this systematic process, which took three years.

"Some people didn't want to be here for anyone else. So, we had to encourage them to leave by helping them see that they would not thrive on our bus. Sometimes you have to stop the bus, let them off, and help them find another bus.

"As we moved through the process, there was turnover. Some were high performers bringing in revenue, but they hurt us long-term. We had a misperception of value. We thought we had a strong team, but it became clear who was and was not in it for the team for the long haul. Some were not going to be a part of our future. We also realized there were rising stars who had been stifled, and we made room for them to grow."

Metrics for Individual, Department, and Organizational Responsibility

To be responsible for their growth, team members and teams need to know where they are on their journey to Peak Performance. We encourage organizations to share Organizational Key Metrics that identify alignment with their Core Identity.

Here are some metrics that clients have directly linked to their Purpose, Vision, and Guiding Principles:

- Purpose and Vision
  - financial: revenues/sales
  - growth in the number of clients/customers/patients/cases
  - rate of on-time delivery
  - new products/initiatives undertaken
- Guiding Principles
  - net profit
  - customer/patient/client satisfaction
  - employee satisfaction
  - scrap/rework

These metrics are indicators of Peak Performance for sustainable success and can be assessed at three levels of the organization:

The **Organizational Dashboard** shares how the organization is operating or functioning at any given time. All team members can see the state of the organization by looking at this dashboard.

The **Department Scoreboard** shows how each department is contributing to organizational success. Each department's operating metrics need to be connected to the Organizational Dashboard.

The **Individual Scorecard** shares how each team member contributes to the department's success and, ultimately, the organization.

Key Objective Metrics clarify and reinforce responsibility for the shared journey, and they tie metrics to the "soft stuff" of the Core Identity.

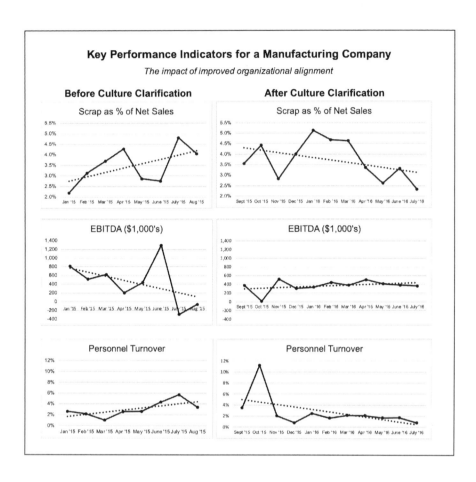

Regular sharing and individual understanding to communicate success or failure are incumbent on everyone. What we consciously and subconsciously focus on is determined by what we measure.

All team members have a role in contributing to this journey. Organizational safety and security come from being on the same page. Success in creating a brighter future depends on all working at their best to support each other. In this way all can feel the responsibility for the journey—together.

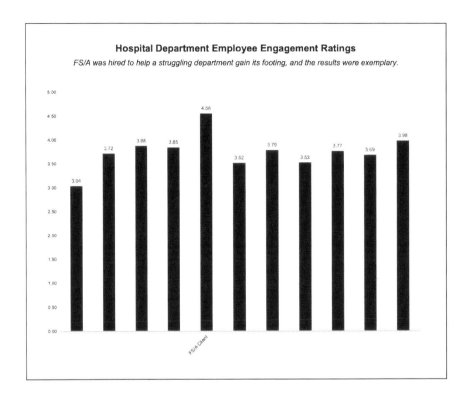

Hospital Department Employee Engagement Ratings

FS/A was hired to help a struggling department gain its footing, and the results were exemplary.

Leadership's Role in Encouraging Bottom-up Alignment

Leadership is ultimately responsible for team success. Leaders are the key enablers of your organization's Reinforcing Systems that create flow for sustainable success. It is leadership's responsibility to close the Peak Performance gaps.

Team members observe what leaders do as well as what they say. They look to leadership to be the role models for acceptable behavior. Furthermore, team members feel the direct impact of what leaders say and do. Most team members assume they should emulate leaders if they want to become leaders themselves or for their own survival in the organization. Strategic, disciplined, purposeful leaders (we'll call them *exemplary* leaders) understand that their actions and words have a ripple effect—they impact the entire organization. What they do and say has the power to create safety and security as team members grow in alignment. Exemplary leaders model the organization's shift from *me* to *team* to help close Peak Performance gaps.

Exemplary *me* to *team* leadership behavior, especially when under pressure, is transformative for an organization.

The exemplary leader on the journey from *me* to *team* views every interaction as an opportunity to reinforce the organization's Core Identity.

Exemplary leaders are aware of the impact of:

- what, when, and how they **speak**

- but most importantly—what, when, and how they **act**

Support of Core Identity Committees

The Core Identity Committees we described earlier require the support of leaders to enable the Reinforcing Systems to permeate the organization. The day-to-day challenges and responsibilities can pull team members away from their committee responsibilities, stalling the institutionalization of the disciplined culture desired by all. It is up to leadership to ensure the success of these committees by encouraging willing and passionate committee members to be leaders helping align the organization.

This is an excellent opportunity to seek and identify the organization's emerging leaders for tomorrow. These high-potential people may leave the organization if not recognized with greater responsibility, and it's an opportunity for emerging leaders to demonstrate their gifts.

Exemplary leaders ensure committees are given the time and resources to institutionalize the desired culture. Furthermore, it's incumbent on the leader to listen and be responsive to the committee's findings and recommendations. Leadership, not the committees, is the ultimate enabler of the reinforcement and the ultimate institutionalization success, and the committees need leadership support.

By sharing responsibility for culture alignment with the committees, exemplary leaders reinforce the shift from *me* to *team*. Exemplary leaders share the responsibility for the journey to creating flow for sustainable success.

We witnessed the comprehensive transformation in an academic health center when the then-authoritarian chair relinquished control of the future of the department to the Core Identity committees. The committees were energized with members from diverse departments and levels, and they met regularly to help create the desired picture of Peak Performance. The transition was dramatic and felt by all. The relinquishing of control created some of the best grassroots work we have seen. As the leader relinquished control, committee members grew in their understanding of leadership, and the department flourished.

Shared Responsibility for Decision-Making

The exemplary leader acknowledges that they do not have all the answers. They are humble and open to learning and growing from any source that can help on the journey. While retaining the ultimate responsibility for decisions made, they seek the best solutions from team members. They are committed to identifying the best possible solution. They seek diverse, balanced perspectives in decision-making. Their experience has shown that the best answers come from team members closest to the challenge who best understand the complexities and implications of the decision. The leader owns the decision but understands that the best decision-making comes from seeking balanced input from many perspectives. If there is a tie on the right thing to do, then the leader may cast the deciding vote.

From the CEO of a consumer products organization:

"My partner and I would develop our game plan for the organization. We'd search for new opportunities, look at acquiring new companies . . . we'd be 90% of the way down the road before engaging our team for input and feedback. They were not in the game, and the execution showed they were not. Now, we may come up with opportunities, but we ask them to investigate with us and help us figure out how good a fit the new opportunity might be. It's helped, and we have gone from an isolation/dictatorship model to a team-oriented model, and it's working."

Exemplary Leaders Give Control

The exemplary leader understands that the intrinsic energy of their team members is the force that will enable the organization to realize sustainable success. Exemplary leaders understand that team members do not want to be average; they desire to be exceptional and set exceptional standards for themselves and others. The exemplary leader giving up control enables team members to own and be responsible for the organization's future. That said, it is also important for the exemplary leaders to continue to support and reinforce the committees, and for team members to sustain their commitment to Peak Performance.

Clarifying Boundaries of the Core Identity

The exemplary leaders and leadership teams help clarify the boundaries of the Core Identity by acknowledging in-bounds behavior and addressing out-of-bounds behavior. And they do so as quickly as possible, so there is no confusion among team members about what is acceptable. The clarified boundaries enable the safety and security all are seeking.

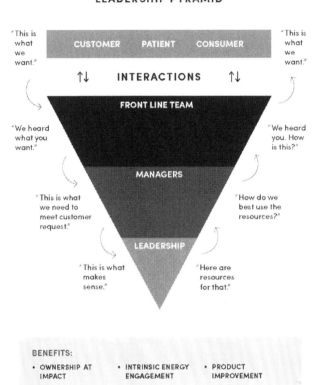

**INVERTED
LEADERSHIP PYRAMID**

"This is what we want."

CUSTOMER   PATIENT   CONSUMER

"This is what we want."

↑↓   **INTERACTIONS**   ↑↓

FRONT LINE TEAM

"We heard what you want."

"We heard you. How is this?"

MANAGERS

"This is what we need to meet customer request."

"How do we best use the resources?"

LEADERSHIP

"This is what makes sense."

"Here are resources for that."

BENEFITS:
- OWNERSHIP AT IMPACT
- INTRINSIC ENERGY ENGAGEMENT
- PRODUCT IMPROVEMENT

One of our clients had identified *care and compassion* as one of their Guiding Principles. In the operating room, a surgeon mistreated and disrespected a nurse, and this violation of a Guiding Principle was called to leadership's attention. Leadership responded by talking to the surgeon, who acknowledged he could do better. This was not the first time this had happened, and he was asked to apologize to the nurse he had mistreated and to the other nurses who had witnessed his transgression. While the breach of Care and Compassion was not fully mended, they could feel headed in a better direction due to the Reinforcing System of the public apology.

People are unhappy when they do not know what is in-bounds and what is out-of-bounds. Even if the feedback is critical, they are happier to know where they stand.

Subtle and Subjective Recognition for In-Bounds Behavior

We find leaders underestimate the power of personal recognition. It is human nature to appreciate positive feedback from leadership, but we are also just as affected by the recognition of others. As a leader, be intentional and purposeful in what you reinforce. Your team is watching when you give feedback, good or bad.

As with formal objective recognition programs, leaders must clarify why someone is being recognized. Be clear when you compliment; do not leave it to others to interpret why you recognized someone. Saying "Good job" is unclear about what was good, and there may be a misinterpretation. Exemplary leaders reinforce alignment by invoking their Core Identity elements in their recognition. In this example, the leader highlights the Guiding Principle of *caring:*

Steve, I am very impressed with how you demonstrated caring for the customer. You stayed positive even when they became short with you. Thank you for displaying who we are at our best, especially when under pressure.

Again, the more intentional and purposeful you are in recognizing aligned behavior, the more the organization's Core Identity is reinforced, and the sooner flow naturally occurs.

Formal and Objective Recognition for In-Bounds Behavior

The leader must use formal and objective recognition strategically to recognize team and team member alignment to the Core Identity for exemplifying the organization at its best. Be purposeful with recognition.

Formal, objective recognition includes these examples:

- perks
- compensation
- promotions/titles
- awards

Most organizations have recognition programs to highlight exemplary performance. To ensure a customized fit for your organization, we recommend tasking a committee with aligning existing recognition programs with the clarified Core Identity and creating new recognition awards if needed.

Fairness (a component of *trust*) is one of humankind's intrinsic shared principles. To honor fairness, perks and compensation must be aligned with the organization's Core Identity. Rewarding anything inconsistent with your Core Identity confuses and de-energizes those trying to align with the Core Identity. The act of bestowing recognition and the reason for doing so is best when communicated clearly and openly.

Too often, recognition is a direct reflection of goal achievement, without regard to how the goal was achieved. One typical example is commission-based sales. *What is the objective that is being rewarded?* If *the sale alone* is being rewarded, and not how the selling was conducted, there can be an impact on future sales. A short-term sales mentality without regard for *honesty* and *integrity* can compromise the organization's brand and threaten its sustainability.

Successful organizations go out of their way to recognize exemplary service that honors the Core Identity. *How* salespeople attempt to make sales is what is valued and recognized. The message is sent that sales are a byproduct of how the organization conducts business when aligned with their Peak Performance Culture. Sustainable sales follow exemplary conduct.

Addressing Out-of-Bounds Behavior

It is natural for humans to test boundaries to clarify what is acceptable and unacceptable so they can feel safe and secure. As a leader, know that boundaries *will* be tested, *must* be tested, and even broken at times for your team to find its comfort zone. Leaders need to understand team members must and will test them, as it is human nature to seek the security boundaries provide.

Team members are trying to understand what you meant by the boundaries you set. Be proactive and help provide clarity on in-bounds and out-of-bounds behaviors.

Respectfully Addressing Perceived Out-of-Bounds Behaviors

Do you ask questions when you perceive the organization's standards are not being met? Do you ask in a way that the team member knows you care about them? Do you care about their development and their role in the organization? Do you understand that as the leader, you are responsible for teaching the proper boundaries, and if they are breached, it reflects your leadership? The leader is responsible for closing the gap in performance and conduct. Asking the right questions enables all parties to be part of the solution.

Organizations that value learning seek and capture teaching opportunities to propel their growth. It is not about what happened in the past, except how we can learn and grow from it. Let's understand why someone thought what they did was right. The following prompts take focus away from the team member's actions and redirect it toward preparation for handling future situations. This isn't about passing judgment—it's about establishing best practices for the future. Leaders can ask:

- I'm confused. Help me understand why you thought that was the right thing to do.
- What could you do differently next time?

- Do you have the tools you need?
- How can I help you?

Addressing Those Not Closing the Performance Gap

What happens when the team member who fails to close their performance gap is allowed to remain as part of the team? Their presence reinforces that leadership is not fully committed to the journey: aligning the organization to Peak Performance.

Furthermore, the team member who is not closing the performance gap is aware of it and knows they are in the wrong garden for them to thrive. They can feel this is not working, and they are stressed and unable to perform or interact as effectively as possible. But many are afraid to make a move themselves. They feel stuck; they need help from leadership.

Aiding the individual to find a better fit reinforces the organization's commitment to caring about the individual and the organization. Both the team member and the organization are beneficiaries.

Time and again, I have had Michigan football players we removed from the team contact me years later to thank me for the wake-up call that changed their lives. They had been directionless. With their removal from the team, they had to take responsibility for their lives. They began building a foundation for a more purposeful and fruitful life.

I used this principle of fit personally in my tough decision to leave Michigan Athletics. Many, including me, thought I was the right person to oversee Michigan Athletics. The President of the university thought otherwise; I was not the fit he was seeking. So, it was time for me to find a different garden to thrive in. No one was wrong—the fit was not right. In the end, I got the chance to pursue this journey to help leaders and organizations realize sustainable Peak Performance. I feel fortunate to have found this special and energizing purpose for my life.

Outcomes of the Shift from *Me* to *Team*

> *From a medical practice client:*
>
> *"When we started working with FS/A, new to-dos were put on our full plate, and it seemed like just one more to-do. Over time, perhaps a couple of years, the to-do's became habits. We look back with wonderment and ask, 'If you do not think this way, how can you possibly make the right decision?' Our mindsets are entirely shifted, and we see a much bigger picture than we saw before we went through this process."*

We Think like a Team

Exemplary leaders encourage and embrace the impact of group decision-making. They are fully aware that the best solutions come from a diverse group of team members collectively guided by their Core Identity. Leadership encourages creative input from team members at all levels of the organization, and they value new ideas. It is never about any one individual. They understand it is about what is best for the organization. They have moved away from seat-of-their-pants decision-making.

We are Envisioning Future Success

There is clarity in where we are going together as each team member is closing the gap on Peak Performance for themselves. Team members at every level are engaged in honoring the organization's Core Identity in how they work together. They are energized by *how* their work moves the organization toward its shared vision for a better tomorrow. A connection between *what I'm doing today* and the *difference we will make together for tomorrow* generates positive feelings. There is comfort and security in knowing the organization is on a trusted, stable journey.

With the shift from *me* to *team* in effect, the clarity of the shared journey comes alive in the mind's eye of every team member. The organization's compelling picture of the desired future is referenced as the star on the horizon. The team knows where the organization is headed, and they are inspired, feeling responsible for their role on the journey.

Envisioning individual peak performance for team success:

University of Michigan Women's Swim Coach Jim Richardson had a psychologist work with his team to help them achieve peak performances. For the team to succeed, each individual must perform at their highest level. The psychologist worked with the team members, asking each swimmer to visualize her perfect swim with a stopwatch in hand. When the gun goes off, envision every stroke and motion perfectly executed to the most minute detail. Feel the water, the power of the rhythmic kick, the movement of each turn, and the power of each push off the wall, and then the finishing touch, clicking off the stopwatch.

Coach Richardson understood the power of the mind in envisioning an emotionally meaningful picture first. This imagined swim was often completed in career-best times. Soon after these vividly imagined swims, some swimmers proceeded to record career-best times.

The more vivid the desired picture in the mind, the more quickly it becomes a reality.

We Create Safety and Security

The desire to feel safe and secure is at the root of human nature. It is a Peak Performance culture that enables team members to feel safe and secure. They know what is expected of all on the team. Team members feel responsible for thinking about the team's best interest, not themselves. They feel a sense of safety and security knowing that team members are looking out for each other. They have each other's backs. Consistency provides an understanding of how decisions are made at all levels of the organization. Leadership values communication and understands that over-communicating is better than under-communicating. Team members feel they are all in the game and are invested in sharing their ideas and feelings, openly giving feedback to support the journey forward.

The members of the two Big Ten Football Championship teams I was part of have always had a close bond. I had thought liking each other and socializing together was always a requirement for building great teams. However, while liking each other inside and outside the office is great, it is not a requirement. The Detroit Pistons proved that.

In the 1990s, the incredibly successful NBA Detroit Pistons team was a great example of living a shared purpose for the team. Powerfully unified team on the basketball court, the Pistons were champions year after year. But when the game ended, they went their separate ways. Although they did not interact outside work, their on-court shared focus was so great they still succeeded.

We Are on a Trusted Journey Together

There is clarity in where we are going together, as each team member is closing the gap on Peak Performance for themselves. Team members at every level are engaged in honoring the organization's Core Identity in how they work together, striving to close their Peak Performance gaps. They are energized by *how* their work moves the organization toward its vision for a better tomorrow. A connection between *what I'm doing today* and the *difference we will make together for tomorrow* generates positive feelings. There is comfort and security in knowing the organization is on a trusted and stable journey.

Our Core Identity Is Our Compass for Dynamic Strategic Planning

With a team culture in place and guided by your Core Identity, your organization can fully tap into its Foundation of Greatness: for each team member, the disciplined responsibility to honor the Peak Performance Core Identity, the competencies to work at the highest level for the job, and the ability to behave appropriately under pressure. Now is the time to engage in Dynamic Strategic Planning for sustainable future success. In Chapter 5, you will set initiatives to close the gap between your Vision and where you are currently, and your Dynamic Strategic Plan will be your map to close that gap.

By undertaking Dynamic Strategic Planning to move toward the organization's compelling Vision, leadership reinforces confidence in the Vision. Team members can feel the integrity of what is said and what is being done.

Questions to Consider

- In hiring, is assessing Organizational Culture Fit your first priority?
- Is your team taking responsibility for alignment with Core Identity? Is leadership?
- Does each team member know their Peak Performance gap? Their department's gap? The organization's gap?
- Are we acknowledging exemplary behaviors and addressing de-energizing behaviors?

Chapter Takeaways

- The organization's culture will be as ingrained as leadership role models the desired culture.

- Not every plant is meant to flourish in every garden. Some on the team are in the wrong garden and need caring help.

- The team created the Peak Performance Core Identity, and they want to be held responsible to that standard.

- We need reminders to help us change old habits, especially when under pressure.

- Stories are the most powerful way to connect with the words and the boundaries of your Core Identity.

- We all have Peak Performance gaps we need to close.

- We need disciplined performance evaluation systems to help us close our Peak Performance gaps.

- Institutionalize Peak Performance behaviors and practices by developing diverse committees staffed by emerging leaders.

- Leadership must be proactive in the alignment process. The organization will go as the team believes leadership wants it to go.

- The result of leadership role modeling and implementing disciplined Reinforcing Systems naturally flows to Peak Performance.

CHAPTER 5

DYNAMIC STRATEGIC PLANNING

Strategy without tactics is the slowest route to victory. Tactics without strategy is the noise before defeat.

—SUN TZU

Understanding what we look like when at our best with a Vision of what we hope to attain provides security for today's decision-making. It also provides the foundation to make decisions for the future. Sustainable success requires clarity about making changes to thrive; how will we adjust and adapt "at our best" to meet our customers' needs tomorrow? We must have our eyes on the future once we have established a stable foundation for today's operations.

Preparing for Tomorrow

We have shared how best to prepare your organization for sustainable success now to enable the organization to compete and thrive in the future. It is about a continual process of creating sustainable success year after year.

Dynamic Strategic Planning

Inspiring Vision → Key Objectives → Objective Key Metrics → Strategic Initiatives

Strategic planning has become a term many organizations give a head nod to but little else. Our work shapes the organization's culture and articulates its Vision to prepare them for a new, more coherent, successful future. This strategic preparation will determine future success or failure. We use the term *Dynamic Strategic Planning* in place of *strategic planning* to emphasize the importance of regular review of the plan and reallocation of resources. The discipline behind Dynamic Strategic Planning for the future will enable sustainability.

To reach its destination—the compelling Vision of a beautiful tomorrow—the organization must find a way to thrive into the future. Doing so will mean anticipating shifting markets and emerging technologies, responding to the needs of an ever-transforming workforce, acquiring resources in a potentially unstable world, and more.

The organization's Foundation of Greatness, as we described in the Introduction, will be its compass for the journey. The Dynamic Strategic Plan will outline initiatives to pursue future success. These initiatives—pathways to the organization's shared Vision—will surface in the planning process as the organization's collective perspectives are engaged.

If the organization commits to this process, it will ensure that the river's natural flow does not get diverted or dammed up. It will be on its way to honoring what it is meant to become.

Compelling Vision

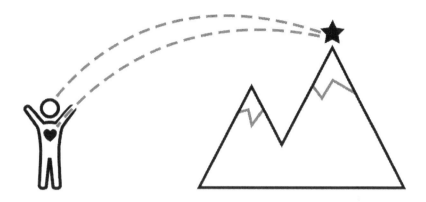

Start with Your Vision: Where Do You Want to Go?

Like a river flowing down a mountainside, organizations that honor their Core Identity feel a natural energy propelling them toward their compelling Vision.

When you plan a road trip, you begin with a destination in mind. You envision the destination and the gap between where you are and where you want to go. You'll need resources like a well-tuned car, gas, food, lodging, and a game plan for reaching the destination. You will need maps and GPS to know if you are on or off course and progress to the destination, and you may need to reroute because of unforeseen obstructions.

Dynamic Strategic Planning is that purposeful process, and it begins with the organization's compelling Vision of a better future for its team members, clients, customers, patients, vendors, and other stakeholders. It establishes objectives of the Vision and identifies initiatives to achieve them.

Be Dynamically Responsive

We must be ready to adapt and adjust dynamically under pressure as we learn more about the status of the course we are on. Be open to adjusting initiatives undertaken as some will produce greater results than others. Resources are limited; where can the best investment be made?

Initiatives do not have guaranteed outcomes. The organization is on a journey that will reveal a clearer destination the closer it gets. As team members go through cycles of Dynamic Strategic Planning, the motivating factor will be a clearer picture of a more successful organization and a clearer picture of the organization's meaningful Vision of a better future.

Commit to a Disciplined Process

In concert with your Reinforcing Systems, Dynamic Strategic Planning prepares your organization to better address tomorrow's challenges by anticipating and getting in front of them. Too often, this planning gets sidetracked by the urgent challenges of the moment, oftentimes challenges that could have been avoided had there been a greater commitment to planning. Too often, excuses for not delivering on long-term plans go unchallenged, and initiatives lose momentum and are soon ignored. We may have invested in a strategic plan, but now it is a binder on the shelf.

The inability to delay gratification is understandable and part of human nature. Humans are wired *to do today*. We all have felt firsthand the immediate gratification of taking on and completing a task. We get satisfaction from actively engaging in activities that bring short-term gratification. We feel the immediate reward of endorphins, dopamine, and adrenaline as we address the "here and now" and feel the joy in checking off tasks accomplished.

Discipline in strategic planning is critical because we receive no immediate gratification from preparing and planning for a better tomorrow. The lack of disciplined planning can jeopardize an organization by leading to a loss of everything it has worked hard to achieve.

For reflection and meaningful planning to occur, new habits must be formed, and future planning must shift from *something that happens when we have time* to a purposeful, ongoing, disciplined system. The Dynamic Strategic Plan must become a living document for reference, examination, re-examination, adjusted to meet the needs of an ever-changing future.

Organizations must develop disciplines to address both immediate challenges and those in the future. We must get used to this way of thinking. Thinking in the now and the future ensures a more predictable and natural flow for success.

Regular, disciplined update meetings are a prerequisite for successful strategic execution. Regularly review key metrics that share where you are on your journey. Set monthly review meetings, if not weekly. Have enough Dynamic Strategic Planning Committee members such that if one or two cannot meet, progress can be made without them.

At each meeting, each committee member shares the status of the deliverable they had committed to the previous week. They also commit to a deliverable for the next meeting.

In simplest terms, the organization fully engaged in Dynamic Strategic Planning:

- Is focused on a shared compelling Vision;
- Has clarity on the objectives of its Vision;
- Is dynamic in assessing initiatives to achieve the objectives and assessing gaps in resources, facilities, habits, systems, talent, skills, and knowledge required to reach its Vision;
- Is disciplined in commitment to strategic progress. The organization does not allow the pressures of the moment and the temptations of immediate gratification to get in the way of a more fruitful journey.

The Process of Dynamic Strategic Planning

The Dynamic Strategic Planning Committee, composed of members representing diverse departments, is tasked with looking years ahead and identifying adjustments for a successful journey toward the organization's Vision. These initiatives can include acquiring new facilities, technologies, staffing, other resources, etc.

Where Are We on the Journey?

The committee may begin by considering the following:

1. Are we communicating effectively about how organizational actions connect to the Vision? If actions are confusing team members, a drop in energy and enthusiasm for the organization naturally occurs. Ensure the following:
   - In introducing new initiatives, connect them to the Vision regularly.
   - Be clear to share the gap between where we are and our Vision.
   - Resolve any confusion about the path to the Vision.

2. Do we have suitable systems in place? Do we have the right people in the correct positions to effectively move the organization toward its Vision? Is leadership aiding team members in closing their Peak Performance gaps?

3. What are our organization's strengths? How can we capitalize upon our competitive advantages—our unique competencies—to move toward our Vision with less effort more effectively?

Dynamic Strategic Planning Engages Your RAS

Start with asking if your shared, compelling Vision is alive in the mind's eye of all team members—this will prepare them to be aware of new, better, more effective ways to serve your clients/patients/customers. Once new objectives are articulated—and time is set aside for intentional reflection on the objectives—the mind's Reticular Activating System (RAS) (discussed in Chapter 2) will ensure that opportunities for adjustments and new strategies for achieving objectives naturally reveal themselves.

What Are Your Vision Objectives?

With an understanding of where the organization currently stands on its Vision journey, leadership and the Dynamic Strategic Planning Committee can define organizational objectives that, when achieved, represent significant progress toward the Vision. These big-picture Vision Objectives bring reality to a Vision that can otherwise seem distant. There must be clarity on how the Vision Objectives connect to the Vision.

Just about any Vision—such as curing cancer, enhancing lives, or creating fulfilled communities—needs objective metrics of success if it is to become a reality. We need to measure progress to our destination. Then we can celebrate successful progress or address shortcomings. The metrics are guideposts on our journey to the destination.

Reveal Gaps

The committee will identify the gaps—what is lacking or inhibiting the achievement of the Vision Objectives? The gaps will generally cluster around funding, staffing, and technology but may include improvements needed in habits around your culture.

If the gaps are within your Core Identity, then the organization is not prepared to undertake Dynamic Strategic Planning. The Core Identity must be in place to journey successfully. Execute Chapters 3 and 4 before venturing to Chapter 5.

Create Initiatives to Close the Vision Gaps

Each department of the organization develops initiatives for closing the gap between where the organization is and the Vision Objectives. The initiatives must include these elements:

- an explanation of the alignment of the initiative to one of the organization's Vision Objectives
- a metric that shares progress toward the Vision Objective
- assets needed for successful implementation
  o budget
  o equipment
  o human resources
- timetable

In addressing these needs for each initiative, the committee should address additional requirements for successful implementation by assessing the following:

- What systems and operational protocols can be improved?
- What habits need improvement?
- What new assets and technologies might aid us in sustaining the journey?
- How can we effectively communicate for all in the organization to know the status of these critical initiatives?

Which Initiatives Will Best Achieve Our Objectives?

Again, diversity of perspective is necessary to best assess the options creatively, holistically, and honestly.

When deliberating the objectives and the initiatives, there may be outliers who see differently or who can imagine what was previously unimaginable. It may seem like their new ideas are coming out of left field, or they might slow the process down. Do not dismiss them. Instead, ask questions and seek deeper insights. Often, outliers see a future for the organization not apparent to others. We have witnessed an organization transform to align with what it is meant to be by adopting an idea from an outlier. Do not rush. Earnest, intentional deliberation will result in a more vital, energizing process.

In assessing which initiatives to pursue, return on investment is your ultimate criterion. To this end, the Dynamic Strategic Planning committee will consider these elements for each initiative:

- budgetary commitment—facilities, equipment, technology, materials, etc.
- staffing commitment
- time frame for successful execution/speed of impact
- impact on the organization, its clients and customers, and the community
- chances of achieving goals

A matrix for objectively assessing and ranking each initiative's value (return on investment) can be created from this criterion. Components for each initiative include selection criteria and corresponding value, criteria competitive rank order, criteria end value, and a return on investment (ROI) score.

Systematizing Dynamic Strategic Planning

Here are steps our clients have taken to incorporate Dynamic Strategic Planning as a disciplined system:

- Create organizational and departmental Dynamic Strategic Planning Committees that represent a diverse cross-section of the organization.

- Hold regular committee meetings (usually monthly, if not more frequently) to assess the status of current initiatives and make resource allocation adjustments.

- Systematize regular communication of progress for the entire organization.

- Honor the meeting time set aside to reflect on current initiatives and future needs.

- Make the Dynamic Strategic Plan a vital part of staff meetings; this culturally reinforces the importance of long-term sustainability over short-term gratification.

- Celebrate accomplishments: Gather the organization to celebrate the successful execution or progress of initiatives.

- When providing updates on metrics, lead with stories that support and convey their impact. While metrics often seem cold and carry little meaning, the numbers are needed to represent concrete progress on the journey.

- Share emotional stories to connect team members to their deeper motivations. Furthermore, meaningful storytelling reinforces the positive actions that led to success, yielding a better chance for future success.

One of our clients seeks to reduce opioid addiction via technology that aids in pain relief. Instead of representing their metrics through sales figures, they calculate addictions avoided and, in turn, lives saved.

Peak Performance

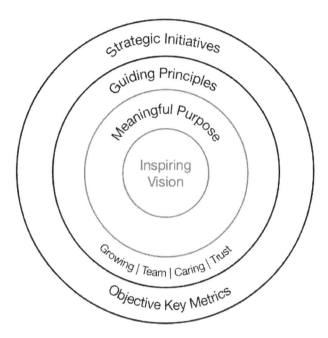

Allan Mullaly was exemplary in using his leadership team meetings to transform the mindset at Ford Motor Company. The meetings had a deliberate dedication to both operations and strategy. You can do the same. Commit to regularly discussing long-term strategy so that doing so becomes a part of your culture. It is what you do because it represents your commitment to the organization's sustainability.

After we introduced this concept to one of our clients, the CEO met with Mullaly to understand how he executed his leadership team meetings. Our client has been remarkably successful in his disciplined dedication to weekly addressing today's operational needs and setting the organization up for future success by reviewing initiative responsibilities and progress. The organization's success is reflected in sales growth over the last eight years—today's sales are four times what they were when we started with them.

Examples of Dynamic Strategic Planning and the Results
Sometimes, We Need to Go Backward to Move Forward

One of FS/A's clients is a successful aftermarket auto parts manufacturer. They develop advanced technology to enhance customers' safety and riding experience. They created a division to bring new technology into the product and manufacturing processes. Despite the innovative technology that had the potential to revolutionize the industry, the division was struggling to meet the company's standards for quality.

The result was intense stress inside the organization. The inability to produce quality products led to plant-wide tension, frustration, and expense. It was de-energizing the entire organization. This went against the company's Vision: *To be known as the suspension company that helped create better lives.* Leadership saw they were not creating better lives for their team members, leading to insufficient progress in helping their customers. As a result, they closed the division.

Leadership honored the organization's Core Identity in making this decision. Their Guiding Principle of respect—*We treat others as they would like to be treated*—helped with their commitment to no employee terminations even though the division closed.

The board of directors later told us this was the first time they had witnessed an organization's leadership make a transformative change that did not require the board's push to do so. Sales of this company have grown 400% in the decade since the division was closed.

Zappos' Dynamic Strategic Planning Leads to a Significant Move

Tony Hseih built Zappos committed to "delivering happiness," and that started with the Zappos employees. San Francisco, where the company was initially headquartered, was so expensive that many employees made difficult, long commutes. Staying true to his Purpose, Hseih moved Zappos to Las Vegas. Not only did Hseih employ a large, eager workforce there, but he also set up headquarters in an underdeveloped area. He made a short-term investment and commitment of $350 million to create a revitalized community that benefited the city and his employees. The foundation for a safe and secure Zappos outlived Hseih, who passed away. However, now a part of the Amazon family, Zappos is strategically set up for a sustainable and successful future.

Patagonia Shifts Focus to Align with Its Purpose

Patagonia was on a roll, growing as fast as they could make products. Then in the mid-1990s, Founder Yvon Chouinard had to make the emotional decision to lay off one-fifth of Patagonia's employees due to the downturn in the economy. Patagonia's primary focus had been on meeting customer demand for their trendy products. He decided to make a dynamic shift in his Vision to impact the planet's sustainable future. Patagonia only uses sustainable materials like recycled polyester, and they create more durable products that don't need to be replaced as often. Both moves were counterintuitive for any finance major. Greater expense and less demand at a higher price! Sounded like a recipe for failure. The result has been anything but that.

Patagonia is in high demand with a stable future. They have a recycling program for their products, and their customers love their commitment to environmental sustainability.

In 2022, Chouinard gave his ownership shares of stock to a not-for-profit to preserve Patagonia's future from the profit pull of public companies. The result is that by ensuring that Patagonia's profits, "the money we make after reinvesting in the business," —according to the brand's statement—will be used to fight climate change. The *Times* pegs these profits at nearly $100 million annually. The impact on climate change can be substantial, and the brand will likely continue to gain devoted followers because of its vision.

Consequences of Lacking Dynamic Strategic Planning and a Clear Purpose

University of Michigan merchandise was becoming very trendy. There was money to be made, so the Michigan Athletic Department went into retail sales. After several years and losing more money than we thought possible, we got out of the business. Selling merchandise was not our expertise; it certainly was not aligned with our Purpose or Vision.

In another example of veering from our purpose, we started a magazine. The public was becoming fascinated with Michigan Athletics and wanted all the information they could get. We decided to provide an inside view with a magazine. Once again, after several years of losing more money than we thought possible, we stopped.

In both cases, we decided to turn over the merchandising and publication to professionals who paid us a fee for the rights. Michigan Athletics now has these streams of income without distraction from its Purpose and Vision.

We were good at developing young people to become impactful citizens of their communities. That's what we did well. *Very well.* Actions aligned with your Purpose and Vision create a natural flow that produces sustainably successful results.

Greatness Unleashed, Greatness Sustained

Through ongoing, systematized Dynamic Strategic Planning, the organization puts itself firmly on the path to sustain that greatness on its journey toward a better future. This is a journey that never ends.

We wish you well, all who choose to go on this deeply meaningful journey.

Questions to Consider

- Is your Vision compelling enough to be a clear guide?
- Do you connect your daily to-do's to your Purpose and ultimately to your Vision?
- Have you clarified the Objectives of your Vision?
- Do you have Objective Metrics that share progress to your Vision?
- Can you identify initiatives that move you to achieve your objectives as you close the gap between where you are and your Vision?
- Do you possess the discipline to attend to the organization's future in times of operational stress?

Chapter Takeaways

- Leadership is responsible for where the organization is headed and what it is doing today.
- Communicate a clear, compelling Vision that all can see and feel.
- The objectives of achieving the Vision must be evident to all.
- Develop well-defined initiatives that move you to achieve your objectives.
- Assess your initiatives for progress toward achieving the objectives.
- Disciplined organizations dedicate time to address the status of initiatives on their journey to becoming all they can be.

CHAPTER 6

LEADERSHIP OF THE FUTURE

A Seismic Change

Before the COVID-19 pandemic, it was a common belief that you could not trust team members to work from home. The significant investment in offices and the supporting systems was considered a requirement—you need to keep an eye on employees to make sure they are productive. While we are still learning about remote work, we are finding we can trust people for the most part. And we are finding that some organizations are more productive with team members working remotely. Team members had long been requesting more freedom to work from home, especially with the advent of families with two working parents. Why could we not see this before the pandemic?

The COVID-19 pandemic initiated a seismic shift to remote work. Like most liberating transformations, there will be future adjustments, but there will be no going back to the old "the office is where all the work gets done" mindset.

The responsibility of the leaders in the future will be the same as it is today: to close the gap between where individuals are performing and Peak Performance for their jobs. When team members are thriving, the organization is thriving. This is how an organization successfully thrives today and will thrive tomorrow. The evolution of human nature has taken thousands of years, and it's not going to change significantly in our lifetimes.

Today, team members expect to be cared for and respected for who they are more than at any time in our history. This is a valued fundamental principle that has always been present, but now there is greater awareness of it. How tomorrow's leaders motivate, inspire, and emotionally engage team members will require changes from the past methods of traditional organizations. The challenge will be respecting and trusting a workforce that has not earned respect and trust the old-fashioned way.

New workforces will increasingly demand to be cared for individually and appreciated for the contribution they can make. Team members will seek greater respect for their earnest commitment to the organization. How can leaders transition from a me-centered mindset that says team members *have to earn the right like the leaders did* to trusting that a team-centered mindset *unleashes untapped energy*?

Our work at FS/A has revealed that there is instinct resident in human beings to do the right thing for the group's greater good. Human nature seeks safety and security. We subconsciously know the larger the aligned community, the safer and more secure we are. In the workplace, team members are asking to be respected for doing the best they can with what they know. And if there is a gap, leadership must provide support to close it.

When the organization understands its Core Identity—its Vision, Purpose, and Guiding Principles—it possesses a framework for decision-making. As a challenge or opportunity arises, a group of three or four team members, providing diverse perspectives, can come together to determine the best course of action. We find this to be true regardless of their rank in the organization's hierarchy. We have found that a small group of aligned team members will set more aggressive goals, more stringent penalties, and tighter timelines than management. We possess an intrinsic desire to be exceptional; none of us seeks to see how average we can be.

For today's job seekers, while pay is still an important factor, other metrics have increasing weight for job satisfaction. Joining an organization with values compatible with one's own set of values in service of a compelling, significant, and gratifying purpose sets the course for sustainable success for both parties. Newer generations are holding out to find work they *feel* good about doing; they have a desire to be intrinsically energized, and they are not wrong to think this way.

Gallup's research on employee happiness has revealed a common desire:

To do deeply meaningful work with people we care about.

Human nature is immensely complicated, but the simple principle of being cared for and respected is surfacing as a prerequisite today. Team members expect to be respected to make the best decision they can and be cared for to help close their Peak Performance gaps.

An expanded definition of respect is evident in the priority many recent college graduates give to environmental sustainability as they assess prospective employers. And we have found that organizations that strongly value respect extend it to the environment and the resources they use—they do not seek shortcuts.

The Internet provides a forum for increasing awareness of *why* an organization exists and how its leaders conduct themselves. While the bad actors gain much attention, exceptional leaders and organizations are being recognized too. Newer members of the workforce have access to more insight into what an organization is striving to become. A shift from *me* to *team* is more critical now than ever for attracting and retaining "A" players who model their Peak Performance culture.

The Team Member of the Future: Expectations

The desire to make a difference, have a positive impact, and do something intrinsically motivating drives young people in their work today more than ever before. They want more than just a job—they want meaning in their life; they want a vocation.

This is a shift from our grandparents' generation when most people felt grateful to have a job. They did what was asked of them because they did not want to risk their livelihood. Their focus was on getting food on the table for the family and a roof over their heads. They did what was asked of them, with little questioning of why.

That is no longer the case for many, and once exposed to a more meaningful culture, it is not easy to go back.

Serving a Higher Purpose

It is uplifting to see the desire of recent college graduates to do something of significance. Many are more passionate about contributing to the benefit of others than making money. A survey by the brand consultancy Calling Brands revealed that working for an organization with a clearly defined purpose is second only to pay and benefits. Two-thirds shared that a *higher purpose* would motivate them to go the extra mile for the organization. Similarly, a survey by social and environmental justice organization Net Impact showed that almost half of today's workforce would take a 15% pay cut to work for an organization with an inspiring purpose.

This change in job motivation is interesting when viewed in the context of the Four Stages of Fulfillment we described in Chapter 2 as we assess our level of maturity.

Stage I Fulfillment: Meeting Our Primary Physical Needs. Many current graduates have not had to worry about their next meal or having a roof over their heads. Primary physical needs can be and often are taken for granted.

Stage II Fulfillment: Learning, Growing, and Competing. Many college graduates have been competing for as long as they can remember. Starting in elementary school, they were graded on academic achievement, whether they made the athletic team, the band, the choir, or the debate team. They have succeeded in the past and possess what it takes to achieve at the next level. They want to be in the big game and experience the feeling of significant personal accomplishment.

Stage III Fulfillment: Benefiting Others. Having had their Stages I and II Fulfillment needs met, many college graduates are inspired by serving a greater purpose than just money. They desire to make a significant contribution to society with the competency built during their years in school. This desire for significance in addressing a societal need at an earlier age than in the past is on the rise—they want to positively impact society right away.

Stage IV Fulfillment: Creating a Better Tomorrow. This is a stretch for young people, and this legacy stage usually is not understood until later in life, perhaps in mature adulthood. Still, many of them are inspired by the stories of young people who have made transformational, long-lasting contributions.

For young people, desiring a higher level of fulfillment is admirable. The concern is that their journey thus far through the jungle of life has not been long enough to have built the foundation of competencies, experiences, and networking connections that are fundamental to making a significant contribution.

The wisest of us cannot list that which we do not know.

Perception is everything, as *we do not know what we do not know*; connecting the dots can seem straightforward. How do leaders inform younger generations that they do not know what they do not know—respectfully? How do leaders do this in terms the young will see as a growth opportunity rather than being put down, thwarted, or disrespected?

There may be no one correct way to inform them that they are not ready for those responsibilities. However, we have found that leaders who genuinely care for (love) their team members can have challenging and life-altering conversations. The caring exchange is about developing the team member. It is about sharing the avenues for them to gain the competencies, connections, and experiences to achieve what is so deeply meaningful to them and the organization.

The answer to why younger generations expect more earlier may be found in a conversation that unfolded at one of our Introduction to the Foundation of Greatness seminars. We ended early one day and asked for thoughts on what the participants had learned. One gentleman asked if it may be possible that the age at which we mature has changed over the last 100–200 years. He explained:

> *Hundreds of years ago, we were much less self-sufficient and more of an interdependent rural agricultural society. We lived on farms or in neighborhoods where we looked after each other because we needed help to survive. You learned to help your neighbor put up their barn or fix their equipment at a young age; you learned you had to be there for each other. So, the sacrifice required for Stage III Fulfillment, Benefiting*

Others, was realized as a young teenager in the past. But today's younger generation desires good feelings although they have not put in the work effort and experienced the delayed gratification required.

Today, we have fences between our homes and hardly know our neighbors. We do not need each other, and we may even be proud that we do not need each other. As a result, maturity may come to us later in life than in the past.

Perhaps today we do not have to grow up as fast as before?

The ensuing animated, open discussion supported that he was onto something. Change is constant, and while we need to learn and grow through the Four Stages of Fulfillment, we must understand that the development opportunities required for advancing from one level to the next most likely has changed over centuries.

Sustainability

In the search for safety and security, today's younger workforce seeks to understand the long-term implications of their organization's decisions. Whether it be for their own welfare, their team members, or the environment, they seek the long-term impact to be positive.

Diverse Perspectives

This new generation has been exposed to diverse opinions and perspectives that provide a better understanding of what they may be creating. Today's students have learned from team or group decision experiences like no previous generation. No longer are they asked to come up with answers on their own; they are challenged to be a part of a team that comes up with the best solutions. They've learned to appreciate the benefit of diverse perspectives in their decision-making. Diversity of thinking is an operational expectation.

Flexible Work Hours, Four-Day Workweek

We find that living the rewarding, meaningful, and thriving life of contribution means much more than the work we accomplish. Our work life may always be our primary driver because it is the economic engine that provides safety and security for our lives. However, people are expecting more from life as they seek time for personal fitness, family activities, and community involvement.

Team members are asking to have their outside-of-work demands respected and to be trusted to accomplish their work. Family demands are real and have always been there, but today the expectation they will be respected and accommodated is greater. At the same time, organizational goals and objectives must be met, but perhaps in new and more unconventional and creative ways.

Unlike in the past, we now see physicians, coaches, and leaders of all kinds taking their children to school in the morning. The number of leaders prioritizing family is unprecedented, and it looks like a movement that will continue. Leaders need to ask, if this caring for family is good for them, should the same opportunity be extended to their team members?

A shortened workweek makes this thriving life of contribution more attainable for many. The challenges of the COVID pandemic opened the door to successful trials of the four-day workweek. In many cases, it is working, and it seems this popular movement will continue.

Side Hustles

Team members understand commitment to the team, but they are not mono-focused. They have many interests and gifts they desire to express and improve. They seek time to broaden their horizon on what the world has to offer them outside of work. We are finding that respect for the outside interests of team members often leads to greater commitment and fulfillment at work. Their life is fuller and more meaningful, and the job has made this broadened perspective possible. They are grateful to have the income from their job while having time to pursue outside interests that increase fulfillment in their lives.

As a leader, how are you adapting to your team members' new and innovative needs so they feel respected and, in turn, may provide you with greater engagement and commitment?

The Subtle Shift for Leaders

New generations with different expectations will bring new challenges to leaders. As outlined in the Attributes of Exceptional Leaders segment in Chapter 3, the expectation to meet these four fundamental attributes will only increase these elements:

- curiosity, with a desire to learn, grow, and understand
- a passion for serving others
- authenticity (building trust with all actions)
- deep caring for team members

That said, one attribute is becoming a more complex and sophisticated requirement for leadership: **deeply caring about team members as they serve the organization**.

Let's help future leaders be better prepared to adjust and adapt to the increasing demand for team members to feel they are cared for, for who and where they are.

The underlying component in all these attributes continues to be humility. Humility permits leaders to get outside of their heads and care about how others are feeling. As shared previously, being a humble servant requires caring about how you make others feel and your impact on their lives. While we never lose our egos, with maturity we experience more meaningful and profound joy from helping others live thriving, valued, and meaningful lives.

We see humble people who make a mistake be forgiven, while those who want to look like they make no mistakes lose our trust. The Internet and technology have provided additional insights into who people are. Leaders who are not truly caring or lack integrity will be found out, and their effectiveness will erode.

Understanding the Desire to Be Cared About

The desire of recent graduates to be cared for and respected is at an all-time high and looks to become even greater. Exceptional leaders understand the many facets of caring, and they know they must adjust and adapt to connect with their team.

While the desire to be respected and cared for has always existed, the demand for respect emerged when workers began to form unions. After unionization was well-entrenched, the shift from *me* to *team* leadership accelerated in the 1960s when college students rejected the top-down authoritarian rule of the times, starting with protests of the Vietnam War. Before this time, widespread dissention over wars in the United States was uncommon. The Vietnam War protests were an affront to the most powerful organization in the world, the US government; the challenge to authority was remarkable. At that same time, college graduates going into the workforce began rejecting the power of large corporations that treated employees like equipment to be manipulated. Since that time, the desire among college graduates to be respected has only increased.

The Perception of Respect and Being Cared About

The challenge for each generation is reconciling its own perspective with those of the previous and succeeding generations. Older leaders earned respect through years of commitment and sacrifice, doing what they were told and keeping quiet. Younger team members are asking to be respected and trusted that they will do the work asked of them. They will work to the best of their abilities, and if they stumble, they expect there will be resources to help them be more successful next time.

Leaders of today and tomorrow are being asked to respect team members before they have earned respect the way the leader had to earn it. Without the volume of proven competency, commitment, or experience, this respect may seem unreasonable to those who had to do more, and wait longer.

So, today's leaders are challenged to move from *me* to *team* by demonstrating caring and respect for new and inexperienced team members. And in more cases than not, we have found that team members surprise leadership with their commitment and dedication to the team effort when respected. They may have a lot to learn but having leaders who care about their growth sets them on a path to be contributors.

The word *love* is little used in business vernacular today, but it is being introduced more and more. Love will surface more in the future as leaders demonstrate their appreciation for team members showing up, giving their best, and caring for each other. Whether the word *love* is used or not, it is the feeling all team members desire as they assess leadership's feelings toward them.

80% Is Not Good Enough

Years ago, when resources seemed to be more limited, decisions were made that would benefit the best interests of 80% of the population or team. At the time, it seemed impossible to accommodate the needs of all; it was too expensive. Today, younger generations expect there to be the resources to accommodate their individual needs and demands.

This will be the greatest challenge for leaders in the future. How can leaders accommodate individual needs while doing what is best for the organization's long-term sustainability? Creativity and collaboration will be vital to accommodate the caring team members of the future will be seeking.

People Are Doing the Best They Can

We ask leadership teams to *assess to what degree they feel others are doing the best they can.* Then we ask them to *assess to what degree they feel they themselves are doing the best they can.* Then we ask: *Why is there a difference between others and you?*

Aren't we all doing the best we can with what we have? We have yet to meet the team member who says, "Let me see how poorly I can perform today," let alone, "I want to see how average I can be." In trying to be the best we can, we are insecure, wishing we were more competent to address our challenges. We all need to accept we do not have all the answers and stop pretending we do.

Each of us is born with unique talents, and then we gain specialized competencies and knowledge on our journey. Effective leaders demonstrate their caring for each team member by respecting that each is doing the best they can with what they have been given, along with their experiences on their life's journey. The leader has the responsibility for and plays a key role in the life journey each team member is on.

Leaders are responsible for supporting the team member in closing their Peak Performance gap. Do they have the tools to do their job, or was there a hiring mistake? Could they better fit in another job? It is not the employee's fault for a poor job fit. Leadership is responsible for hiring the right people and then closing the Peak Performance gaps with proper orientation, coaching, training, and resources for team members to do their best work. It is through adding the team members' perspectives to those of the leader's that the organization realizes Peak Performance.

By respecting that team members are doing the best they can from their perspectives, the leader plays a vital role when they acknowledge contributions. When we feel good about our contribution, we are motivated to do even more to become better. We feel good about ourselves and are gratified to be appreciated for our contribution, even if there are gaps we are working on.

Leaders Build Relationships

Great leaders today and, more increasingly, tomorrow will need to be relationship builders inside and outside the organization. These relationships start with caring about and respecting team members at all levels of the organization. A key to caring and relationship building is understanding our emotional intelligence.

Psychologists who study emotional intelligence, including Peter Salovey, Robert Sternberg, and Daniel Goleman, describe it as the ability to identify, understand, and manage emotions. Emotional intelligence includes the following elements:

- **self-awareness** – the ability to identify and name one's own emotions as they happen, and understand the links between thoughts, feelings, and reactions
- **self-management** – the ability to manage one's emotions, including, for example, by self-soothing, and the ability to harness emotions in service of a goal
- **social awareness** – the ability to identify and understand emotions in others, understand subtle social signals, and be empathetic
- **relationship management** – the ability to understand how others feel, and then behave in a way to shape those feelings; the ability to listen well and ask good questions

How we make others feel impacts a team member's ability to think and act. Starting with our self-awareness that we are doing the best we can and are open to learning and growing, we can be vulnerable on our journey to deeply care about team members. In doing so, team members will learn they are in a safe, secure place. When there is deep caring from the leader, it is an emotional feeling of being seen, heard, and understood. The leader's words are not as important as the leader's emotions and feelings. New leaders who deeply care can jump in vulnerably and stumble with the words, but the caring will be felt and understood. This is a foundation for the intrinsic stability of your team.

Be Curious; Be Open to Learning and Growing

We conclude with the essential attribute of exceptional leadership—the desire to learn and grow, to be better tomorrow than today.

Leadership is not about having the answer; it is about enabling the best solution. None of us know as much as we would like when making decisions. That said, the leader is responsible for the decision. The desire to humbly learn and grow and admit that we do not have all the answers is vital for great leadership.

The first time I had an IT specialist help me with a computer problem, I was surprised to find him searching online for a solution. He knew the question to ask; I did not.

When others see a situation differently, great leaders are curious about the reasons. Do they know something the leader does not, or was there miscommunication in the past? Great leaders speak 10–25% of the time during a discussion, mostly asking questions that challenge others to think.

Leadership is not about having the answer; it is about enabling the best solution.

For us to operate at Peak Performance, we need the best knowledge available. Creating an environment where all are learning from each other sets the stage for building a learning organization, an organization that, at its foundation, says: *We do not have all the answers, and we are open to learning and growing.* It starts with leadership shifting from having the answers to knowing the questions to ask, shifting from *me* to *team.* It is those who are humble on their journey, curiously in search of better understanding, who will be able to do the following:

- close the gap on becoming the leader they are meant to be by being open to the growth opportunities team members provide
- become the leader their team needs by listening and reflecting on what is working and what is not
- create a culture where the team members support each other in learning and growing to close personal Peak Performance gaps, all in service of making the team better
- create an organization that possesses a competitive edge as they are constantly learning and growing

The Core Purpose of Leadership: Close the Peak Performance Gap

We emphasize that the key metric for leadership is closing the Peak Performance gap for each team member. Then and only then can the team realize Peak Performance.

Responsibility to others is the foundation of Stage III Fulfillment: Benefiting Others. It is supported by the good feelings we get from helping others thrive. It is our supporting, mentoring, and coaching others to go places they could not go by themselves. While leaders may not get short-term gratification from helping team members grow, they experience a much deeper satisfaction from knowing that the person they are supporting will make their own life, and perhaps the lives of others, better with the help the leader provided.

As shared previously, each team member is doing the best they can. Leadership is responsible for recognizing their effort. If they are not meeting the growth desired to move toward Peak Performance, leadership must look in the mirror, taking responsibility for these factors:

- Is this person a good culture fit for our team?
- Did they have the competency or the potential to do this job when hired?
- Did we understand whether their behavior under pressure was a good fit for this job?
- Are they in the proper position, or is there a better job fit?
- Do they understand what Peak Performance is for this job?
- Have we trained them for Peak Performance on this job?
- Have we given them the tools to perform at the expected level?
- Are we modeling how we expect them to work with others?

Good leaders blame themselves for poor hiring; it is not the hired person's fault if they were set up to fail. Good leaders take responsibility, taking the blame for poor fit, and giving credit to the team member when they succeed.

Questions to Consider

- Does your organization make it clear that you are in business for the long term, committed to building a sustainable future?
- Are you open to caring for and respecting younger generations who may not have had to work as hard as you did to be respected?
- As a leader, do you respect that each of your team members is doing the best they can with what they have been given?

- When one of your team members fails or struggles, do you assess your contribution to their struggle?

- Do you understand the Peak Performance gap for each of your direct reports and frequently provide support in closing that gap?

Chapter Takeaways

- As we are seeing with today's workforce, future team members will seek to have personal needs respected, enabling them to be more fully engaged. This desire to be individually cared about and respected is surfacing as they seek a workplace that features these elements:
  - meaningful work that makes a difference
  - environmental sustainability
  - diversity of perspectives
  - flexible work hours
  - the opportunity to take time for secondary side hustles

- Fundamental characteristics of leaders of the future (humility is the common thread) include the following:
  - curiosity, with a desire to understand, learn and grow
  - a passion for serving others
  - authenticity (building trust with all actions)
  - deep caring for team members

CLOSING

Our experiences are supported by research on how we can best thrive together, not just survive. Human nature is much more complex than we may ever completely understand. Leaders who serve a greater Purpose, and who appreciate and respect the Foundation of Greatness that resides in each team member, possess the vital ingredient for sustainable success. They have made the shift from *me* to *team*.

While the philosophers Socrates, Aristotle, and Plato may have been the first to document the study of human nature and our motivations, there has been a remarkable deepening in the understanding over the last fifty years. We continue to be energized by learning from clients and the vast research coming out of academia, like the University of Michigan's Center for Positive Organizations at the Stephen M. Ross School of Business and others.

While there is an unending deepening of our understanding of sustainable greatness, the fundamentals we share in this book provide the foundation for all of us individually and collectively to live thriving lives for sustainable success.

We hope this book helps you simplify the complexity of leadership. *The Shift from Me to Team* shares insights from the great leaders we have witnessed lead organizations to sustainable success, Peak Performance, and greatness. We find this is an energizing and rewarding journey we are honored to be on with you.

Thank you for the opportunity to support you on your journey.

APPENDIXES

Appendix A: Extraordinary Teams Survey: Beyond High Performance

Adapted from works by organizational change consultants Shawn Quinn and Don Mroz

Rate your feeling on a scale of 1–5 *with 1 being poor and 5 being great. Your response will be confidential; we appreciate openness.*

1. _____ We have a clear purpose.

2. _____ We actively and consciously look for the positive in what we are doing.

3. _____ We celebrate success regularly.

4. _____ We seek to understand what created the successes we have had as a team.

5. _____ We hold each other accountable for producing results that will move us toward our purpose.

1. _____ I understand how what I do affects the team's Purpose.

2. _____ I feel comfortable sharing ideas with the team.

3. _____ I feel risk-taking is encouraged on this team.

4. _____ I feel valued as a part of this team.

5. _____ I am regularly encouraged to come up with new ways to do my job.

6. _____ I have a chance to share what I have learned as part of my job with the team.

7. _____ I know my role on the team.

8. _____ I have passion for what I am doing.

9. _____ I am known for my strengths and allowed to use them.

Appendix B: Peak Performance Assessment Template

Peak Performance Assessment for _____

Peak Performance = Culture Fit + Competency Fit + Behavior Fit

Please rate your team member on each component of the Peak Performance Evaluation. Please provide real examples exemplifying the rating given to create the most accurate, effective picture possible for the team member. Please add an Objective Key Metric (OKM) for each, if possible.

Ratings: 1–10, with 1 = does not fit at all; 5 = fits, as much as does not fit; 10 = perfect fit **OR** A = Role Model; B = Can become a Role Model; C = Unlikely to become a Role Model

Organizational Culture Fit

Purpose Alignment   *OKM* _____   Rating: _____

Purpose _____

Examples _____

Vision Alignment   *OKM* _____   Rating: _____

Vision _____

Examples _____

Core Values Alignment

Core Value A Alignment *OKM* _____   Rating: _____

Core Value A _____

Examples _____

Core Value B Alignment *OKM* _____   Rating: _____

Core Value B _____

Examples _____

Core Value C Alignment *OKM* _____   Rating: _____

Core Value C _____

Examples _____

Core Value D Alignment *OKM* _____   Rating: _____

Core Value D _____

Examples _____

Core Value E Alignment   *OKM* _____   Rating: _____

Core Value E _____

Examples _____

Job Competency Fit

Natural Talents Needed (list and rate each)

OKM _____

Natural Talent Needed	Rating	Examples that support the scoring

Learned Skills Needed (list and rate each)

OKM _____

Learned Skills Needed	Rating	Examples that support the scoring

Knowledge Needed (list and rate each)

OKM _____

Knowledge Needed	Rating	Examples that support the scoring

Job Behavior Fit

Purposeful Behaviors   *OKM* _____   Rating: _____

Examples _____

Positive Energy   *OKM* _____   Rating: _____

Examples _____

Passion for the Job   *OKM* _____   Rating: _____

Examples _____

Appendix C: Resources for the Reader

Center for Positive Organizations, University of Michigan Ross School of Business

"The Center for Positive Organizations is dedicated to building a better world through the science and practice of thriving organizations."

https://positiveorgs.bus.umich.edu/an-introduction/

Everybody Matters

"We're showing what's possible at the intersection of great business strategy and profound care for people."

https://www.barrywehmiller.com/home

WorkLife with Adam Grant (podcast)

"Organizational psychologist Adam Grant takes you inside some truly unusual places, where they've figured out how to make work not suck."

https://adamgrant.net/podcast/

Simon Sinek

"We're here to provide you with the tools to inspire every single member of your team."

https://simonsinek.com/all-things-business/

Jon Gordon

"Inspiring people and organizations to work with more vision, passion, positivity, and purpose."

https://jongordon.com/books/

The Knowledge Project with Shane Parish (podcast)

"We interview world-class doers and thinkers so you can better analyze problems, seize opportunities, and master decision-making."

https://fs.blog/knowledge-project-podcast/

ABOUT THE AUTHOR

For more than twenty years, Fritz Seyferth and his team at FS/A have been helping organizations access their untapped potential, paving the way for achieving consistent, sustainable Peak Performance. By combining a systems engineering mindset with a deep understanding of human motivation, Fritz shares how a meaningful life is enhanced when we partner with like-minded people who make the shift from *me* to *team.*

Fritz learned early in life to be flexible and open to change, and to understand there are many ways to succeed: He lived in seven cities in five states before starting kindergarten in Covina, CA, and then moved to Swarthmore, PA, before settling in Darien, CT, where he finished high school.

Understanding how things work—and taking them apart and putting them back together to work even better—has always been a fascination for Fritz, whether it is a bicycle, plant layout, or organization.

He was fortunate to compete at the highest levels in college, as a professional athlete, and in business. His more than forty-year study of leadership and exceptional teams has provided an intimate understanding of the principles and disciplines found in the most successful leaders and organizations.

These experiences comprise the foundation for his deep understanding of exceptional leaders and the strategies for consistently surpassing expectations:

- playing football and earning his Industrial/Operations Engineering degree at the University of Michigan
- playing professional football for the New York Football Giants and Calgary Stampeders
- attending night school at four universities to earn his MBA
- working as a consultant with BF Goodrich in Akron, Ohio, and Arthur Young & Co. in New York City
- holding leadership positions, including Executive Associate Athletic Director, for twenty-one years in the University of Michigan Athletic Department
- creating a Tier-2 automotive manufacturing company and a biotech company
- leading the FS/A Team Building/Leadership Development practice

In Fritz's long-term commitment to the Ann Arbor area, he has supported thirteen non-profit boards and many for-profit boards, and he has built a reputation as a confidant with unquestioned trust and commitment to those who serve others.

Outside of his coaching practice and being with family, Fritz's passions are woodworking, being out-of-doors hiking, rowing the Huron River, mountain biking, road biking, snow skiing, and all activities on the water with the grandkids at the family summer home in Traverse City, Michigan.

Fritz resides in Ann Arbor with his wife, Lynn, and cherishes his relationships with his three children and twelve grandchildren.

INDEX

20/60/20, 96
   alignment ratio, 100
   natural fit ratio, 84–86
360° assessments, 125

A

"A" players, 14
absenteeism, 1
abundance, 57
accidents, 1
accomplishment(s), 55
   celebrate, 152
   personal, 163
   and recognition, 46
   short-term, 47, 123
   signs of, 45
adaptable/adaptability, 57
adolescence, 45, 47
adrenaline, 42, 43, 58, 123, 146
adulthood, 49, 153
Akron, Ohio, 25
alignment,
   beginning, 38
   five stages of cultural, 37
   intellectual and emotional, 38
analysis, 24

anger, 58
Ann Arbor, 48, 55, 186
answers, 11
Arthur Young & Co, 25, 27, 28
assess and decide, 24
assessment, behavioral, 41
assets,
    providing the required, 16
    underutilized, 25
    unique set of, 16
Aristotle, 3
attitude, positive, 23
authenticity, 57, 71, 72, 77, 81, 97,
    167, 175
awards, 114, 135
awareness, 7, 57, 89, 160, 161
   self-, 171, 172
   social, 171

B

balance, 57
beauty, 53, 57
Belkin, Deb, 59
benefiting others, 42, 44, 47–50. *See also*
    four stages of development
behavior,

appropriate, 16
out-of-bounds, 136–137
belief(s) that/in/about,
    fundamental selfishness of humans,
       50
    misguided, rooted in history, 8
    our actions today will create a better
       tomorrow, 51
    organization positively impacts
       people's lives, 17
    team members can't be trusted to
       work from home, 159
    what attributes great leaders possess, 8
Berenson, Red, 104, 105
BF Goodrich, 25, 28
Big Ten Conference Championship, 6
Big Ten Football Championship, 140
boards of directors, 17, 154
brain,
    executive, 13, 39, 40
    limbic, 57
    primitive, 13, 39, 40
    and muscles work better, 78
Built to Last, 29
Burton, Tirrel, 27
business strategy/strategies, 58, 183
businesses, most sustainably successful, 29

C
Calgary Stampeders, 25
Cameron, Kim, 61
capital assets, 53
caring, 23, 25, 37, 56, 60, 62, 63, 64,
    66, 68, 69, 71, 76, 78, 80, 81, 82,
    95, 97, 102, 110, 112–113, 124,
    134, 137, 141, 164, 166, 167, 168,
    169, 170, 171, 172, 174, 175
challenges, 21
change, 84, 110

in atmosphere, 84
growth and, 95
habits that didn't, 123
habits that need to, 65, 101
the lens through which team mem-
    bers view the organization, 86
old habits, 101, 142
open to, 185
organizational, 179
requirements for the organization
    to, 92
resistance to, 13
seismic, 159–167
significant, 79
transformational, 57, 103
transformative, 103, 154
Cherry Republic, 40, 41
Chouinard, Yvon, 155
Cipa, Larry, 6
civilization survival, 28
classical economic theory, 50
climate change, 155
coach, 6, 27, 30, 48, 59, 63, 64, 70,
    104, 105, 124, 139
coaching,
    high-quality, 23
    leaders, 71
    Peak Performance and, 74, 75, 170
    practice, 186
    staff, 7
    supporting, mentoring, and, 173
    training and, 16
co-creation, 13
collaboration, 57
    communication and, 60
    creativity and, 170
    value of, 54
    and teamwork, 58
Collins, Jim, 28

commitment, 2, 23
communities, of interdependent people, 9
community,
    acting in best interest of our, 50
    greater safety and security for our, 50
    of independent contractors, 37
    survival and growth of the, 28
    sustainability of, 37
compassion, 57, 59, 60
    care and, 133, 134
compensation, 45, 46, 135
competencies, 15, 47, 48, 58, 111, 141,
    148, 163, 164, 70
competition, 50
competitive advantages, 148
compliance, intellectual, 38
conflict, 57, 65
confusion, 30
Connecticut, 25, 26
Conversational Intelligence, 13
contentment, 48, 51
contributions, recognized and valued,
    17, 19
Core Identity,
    align organization to its, 95, 113
    aligning existing recognition pro-
        grams with, 135
    aligning operational systems to the, 123
    alignment with, 107, 109, 111, 118,
        123, 135, 141
    assessment of fit with the, 56–57
    behaviors that align with the, 104
    clarified, 94, 95
    clarifying the, 67, 70, 81, 103
    clarifying boundaries of the, 132
    clear to all team members, 66
    committees, 113, 114, 116, 117, 130, 131
    components of, 18, 38–40, 70
    Culture Clarification process and, 99

critical failure factors and, 93
culture that honors your, 39
deep, 71
as enabler of sustainable greatness,
    35–66
enables flow, 36–38
exemplary leaders and, 134
Dynamic Strategic Planning and, 141
feelings and, 66, 86
gaps within your, 149
Guiding Principles and, 56, 87
honoring your, 91–93, 103
honoring the organization, 66, 112,
    140, 145, 154
leadership and, 70, 154
meaningful, 71
need to articulate a clear, 41
organization's, 86, 100, 108, 130,
    134, 138
as organization's compass, 113
organization strayed from its, 110
Organizational Key Metrics that
    identify alignment with, 127
Peak Performance, 15, 112, 119, 142
process to reveal and clarify, 18
recognition of exemplary service
    that honors, 135
reinforcing the, 93, 107, 115, 117
reinforcing systems and, 36, 101
revealing the organization's, 36
revealing your, 84
rooted in deep and meaningful
    Purpose, 39
shared, 35, 39, 85, 91, 118
stories and, 142
systems not aligned with, 123
team engagement process and, 70
team member alignment to the, 134
team member honoring the, 126

team members acknowledged and
recognized for exemplifying
the, 113
team members collectively guided
by their, 138
third component, 56–58
understanding of the, 96, 160
violations of the 109
that will guide organization's work
far into the future, 67
corporate America, 8
cortisol, 13, 42, 58
courage, 57
COVID pandemic, 1
challenges of, 166
four-day workweek and, 166
remote work and, 80, 159
lack of management tools before, 1
create a better tomorrow, 18, 42, 44. *See
also* four stages of development
creativity, 13, 57
and collaboration, 170
enhanced, 104
and innovation, 78
required for innovative productivity, 9
restricted, 104
Critical Failure Factors, 93, 97, 113,
115. *See also* Essential Success
Factors
Csikszentmihalyi, Mihaly, 5
culture,
adoption, 115
alignment, 37, 131
assessment, 118
and Behavior Fit, 109
built on an ideal greater than any
individual, 7
clarification, 10, 18, 30, 36, 41

committee, 114
compromised, 109
Core Identity and, 141
disciplined, 130
employees who are a challenge to
the, 14
where everyone feels safe and
secure, 17
Fit, 115, 117, 119, 120, 124, 174,
180
Fit, Organizational, 109, 111, 117,
118, 119, 124, 126, 141, 181
habits around your, 149
honoring the organization's, 120
that honors your Core Identity, 39
institutionalization of the, 107, 113, 130
leaders need to know the organizational, 9
leadership role modeling the
desired, 141
that leads to having a sustainable
impact on others' lives, 19
that leads to thriving, 19
long-term strategy and your, 153
meaningful, 162
misaligned Reinforcing Systems
and, 110
of mistrust, 14
Peak Performance, 99, 103, 114,
121, 135, 139, 162
reinforcing systems and, 36, 37
shared team, 107
where team members support each
other, 173
thriving, 10
that unleashes the team's greatness, 10
that values and recognizes everyone's contributions, 17
work shapes the organization's, 144

Culture Clarification, 67–97
   interviews, 110
   process, 30, 36, 41, 84, 87, 91, 95,
      99
Culture Clarification retreat, 10, 51, 53,
   67, 68, 69, 70, 80, 82, 83, 113
Culture Fit, 86, 109, 111, 115, 117,
   118–120, 124, 126, 141, 174, 180,
   181
curiosity, 19, 24, 56, 71, 74, 81, 82, 95,
   96, 167, 175

D
dashboard, 127
decision-making,
   better, 11
   from the bottom up, 9
   flow, 28
   foundation for, 8, 15, 16, 18
   Guiding Principles and, 35, 57
   organizational, 19
   Peak Performance and, 36
   primitive mammalian brain and, 13
   reactive, 39
   shared responsibility for, 131–132
decisions,
   good and bad, 11, 15
   how we make, 16
dedication, 2, 57, 60
   commitment and, 169
   deliberate, 153
   disciplined, 153
de-energized, 19
defects, work with, 1
deficiencies, unique set of, 16
determination, 57
diversity,
   of knowledge, 83
   of opinions, 72

   of perspectives, 150, 175
   power of, 111–112
   of thinking, 165
dopamine, 42, 43, 58, 146
Dynamic Strategic Planning, 18,
   143–157
   Committee, 147, 148, 149, 151
   consequences of lacking, 156
   Core Identity and, 141, 149
   examples and results of, 154
   importance of regular review and, 144
   motivation for, 146
   organization fully engaged in, 147
   process of, 148–156
   sustainability and, 144
   systematizing, 151–153, 156
   tomorrow's challenges and, 146
   Vision and, 145
   and your RAS, 148
   Zappo's, 154

E
economic engine, 166
economic theory, 50
educators, 49,
ego, 45, 46, 47, 77
electronic media, 53
Elliott, Bump, 24
emotions, 39
empathy, 13, 60
Employee engagement,
   decline in, 1
   Gallup 2021 survey, 1
   model for, 72
endorphins, 43
energized, 19
energy, 9
   collective well of untapped, 17
   contagious, 39

generative, 40, 48, 58
intrinsic, of people, 25
level of the workforce, 25
positive, 56
short-term, 42
sustainable, 40
team's collective, 40
untapped intrinsic, 24–25
engagement,
    employee, 1, 72
    lack of, 9
    optimal, 5
entrepreneurship, 57
environment,
    long-term positive impact on the,
        165
    meaningful, for highest value ser-
        vice, 89
    for mutual learning, 173
    that prevents natural greatness to be
        tapped, 14
    respect extended to the, 161
    for thriving at work, 1
Essential Success Factors, 91–93, 97,
    113, 115. *See also* Critical Failure
    Factors
executive coach, 30
expectations, high, 22
    setting, 23
experiences, 16
    writing down energizing, 32

F
fairness, 56, 57, 135
family, 22, 57, 80, 162, 186
    activities, 166
    demands, 166
    life, 123
fear, 13

feeling(s),
    allowing expression of, 88–89
    appreciation of perspectives and, 82
    being genuinely valued, 69
    caused by good hormones, 78
    collective, 95
    Core Identity and, 66, 86
    count, 82
    and decision-making, 86
    and decisions in organization's best
        interest, 65
    depleted, 16
    emanate from our brains, 39
    energized, motivated, and alive, 16
    good, 165, 173
    hope and, 95
    in foundational stories, 21
    generated by trust and caring, 62
    intrinsic, 57, 101
    knowing team members', 110
    leader's, 172
    leader valuing, 95
    leadership's, 169
    leadership's sensitivity to, 59–60
    Peak Performance and, 66
    positive, 138, 140
    reflection on, 43
    relationship management and, 171
    resident in the organization, 68
    respect for, 89
    reveal who we are, 21
    right, 43
    role of, 58–60
    of safety and security, 110, 112
    self-awareness and, 171
    sharing, 70, 82, 95, 140
    stories and, 86
    storytelling and, 86
    tangible, 95

team's, 69, 70
today's younger generation and, 165
understanding of, 87
your values and your, 33
from words to, 102
fight, flee, or freeze, 13
Fisher, Steve, 59
flexible/flexibility, 57
flow, 27–28
    Core Identity enables, 36–38
    culture alignment and sustainable, 37
    definition of, 5–8
    enablers of, 8, 19
    energized, 19
    energizing, 36, 38
    example of the essence of, 7
    feeling of, 7
    five stages of organizational, 37–38
    greater, 43
    natural, 59
    operating in alignment with prin-
        ciples and, 58
    of our work, 33
    successful, sustainable, 35
    sustainable success and, 36, 38
    in work, 43
football, 5–8, 24, 25
Ford, Gerald, 73
foresight, 13
Fortune 50 companies, 26
foundation,
    building of our, 15–16
    stories that reveal our, 17
    for sustainable success, 15
Foundation of Greatness,
    alignment with shared Core Identity
        and, 35
    capitalizing on your, 106–107

in each team member, 17, 19, 62,
    177
    components of, 15–16
    critical components of, 29, 32
    deeper understanding of, 15
    definition, 8
    individual, 106
    organization's, 106, 144
    origin of the term, 28
    our, 13–15
    and Peak Performance, 8
    principles, 29
    retreat on Unleashing Your, 43
    seminars, 164
    sustainable success and, 32
    system, 29
    team culture, Core Identity, and 141
    understanding your, 106
"Four Levels of Happiness," 41
four stages of development, 44
Four Stages of Fulfillment, 41–52, 163,
    165
frustration, 2, 58, 68, 154
FS/A, 8, 14, 29, 55, 56, 82, 102, 138,
    154, 160, 185, 186
    culture process, 12, 83
    Foundation of Greatness and, 106
    Four Stages of Fulfillment, 41–52
    goals, 17
    instinct to do the right thing and, 160
    journey to unleashing Greatness
        and, 17
    leaders' insecurities and, 15
    performance reviews and, 121
    process to reveal and clarify the
        Core Identity, 18
fulfilled, 19
fun, 57
    with others, 31

G

Gallup's 2021 employee engagement survey, 1

generations, 46, 52, 90
  future, 8, 51, 76
  new/newer, 161, 167
  previous and succeeding, 168
  working together, 90
  younger, 164, 169, 174

generosity, 57

genuineness, 57

gifts, 16
  appreciation of our, 21
  that are most important for author, 22
  collective, 9
  individual unique set of, 11, 15
  journaling and your, 32

Gittell, Jody Hoffer, 61

Glaser, Judith, 13

gratification, 41, 106
  delayed, 42, 44, 165
  ego, 47
  immediate, 53, 146, 147
  inability to delay, 44, 146
  short-term, 19, 43, 146, 152, 173

greatness,
  achieving, 17
  enabling of individual, 9
  enablers of sustainable, 8, 18, 35–66
  foundation of, 8, 13–14, 19
  journey toward sustainable, 36
  journey to unleashing, 17–18
  leadership's role in, 28
  organization's, 22
  sustainable, 8, 13, 28, 29, 35–66
  revealing the, 67–97
  that resides in each team member, 19
  that resides in your organization, 18

unleashing, 8

growing, 24, 57, 100, 103, 106, 124, 155, 163
  feedback on how we are, 122
  in the job, 120
  open to learning and, 131, 172–173
  together, 72

growth, inspiring continued, 16

Guiding Principle(s), 12, 23
  caring as, 23, 60, 133
  clarifying, 56
  clarifying boundaries of, 64–65, 96, 103–104
  as compass for decision-making, 35
  compassion as, 133
  Core Identity and, 91, 111, 113, 117, 118, 160
  Culture Clarification process and, 99
  decision-making and, 57
  exist to serve the Purpose, 80
  Foundation of Greatness and, 15
  hiring and, 115
  integrity, 23
  metrics linked to, 127
  most compelling, 56
  nonoptional, 62
  organization's, 36, 56
  organizational culture fit and, 118, 120
  popular, 57
  reinforced and honored, 59
  Reinforcing Systems and, 100
  relationship boundaries and, 57
  referencing our, 66
  revealing components of, 70
  revealing the organization's, 87–88
  role of, 58–60
  shared, 18, 118
  transition from words to practice, 92
  trust as, 60

trust and caring as imperative, 66
voting for deciding components of,
    68, 70
what they do, 57–58
for working at our best together,
    56–58

H
habits,
    aligning, 107
    better, 18, 92, 109
    bad, 14, 108
    Dynamic Strategic Planning and,
        147
    more purposeful, 40, 96, 97
    that need improvement, 150
    needed to change, 65
    new, 40, 84, 96, 100, 109, 113, 147
    old, 65, 97, 101, 103, 108, 142
    patience and changing, 101
    performance evaluations and, 121
    peril of reinforcing bad, 109–110
    stress and, 123
    to-do's and, 138
    around your culture, 149
    See also Reinforcing Systems
happiness,
    delivering, 154
    employee, 161
    "Four Levels of," 41
    hormones, 42, 58
health, 43
hiring,
    dimension to assess in, 30
    process, 56
    the right person, 16
    the wrong people, 56
home life, 2
honesty, 57, 60, 84, 135

honor,
    tradition, 7
    who we were meant to be, 16
hormones,
    happiness, 42, 58
    stress, 13, 42, 58
human beings,
    are meant to work together, 3
    are wired to be moved by team
        success, 9
human,
    desire for sustainable greatness, 13
    nature, 3, 5, 13, 29
    principles, 2
human desire,
    to belong to a community, 9
    to succeed as a team, 9
humility, 57, 71–73, 77, 96, 167
    leaders of the future and, 175
    and vulnerability, 74

I
ideas, make sense of, 24
Identity,
    Core, 18
    Peak Performance and Core, 15
    unique, 21
impact,
    of frustration in team members, 2
    of giving power to the team, 12
    positive on boards of directors, 17
    of thousands of WWII officers, 8
    transformative and meaningful, 18
innovation, 56, 57, 78
insecurity, 15, 65
insight, 13
integrity, 23, 57, 62, 77, 117, 124, 141
    and caring, 23
    as component of trust, 60

culture fit and, 117
honesty and, 135
of individual lives, 60
leaders who lack, 168
isolation, 58, 132
issues, 57, 100

J

jealousy, 58
Job Behavior Fit, 117, 120–121, 124, 183
Job Competency Fit, 117, 118, 119–120, 182
Jobs, Steve, 22
journaling, 32

K

Kelleher, Herb, 61
kindness, 57, 62, 78
Knickerbocker Toy Company, 26
knowledge, 15, 16, 45, 47, 83, 86, 119, 120, 124, 147, 170, 173, 182, 184

L

leaders/leaders',
authoritarian, 9
attributes of great, 8
collective gifts and, 9
collective intelligence and, 9
collective talents and, 9
collegiate head football coaches as, 23–25
control and, 132
curiosity about organization and its culture, 9
deep sense of fulfillment, 9
effective, 13, 14
essential attributes for tomorrow's, 18
exceptional, 25, 63, 71–83, 96, 161, 167, 168, 186
exemplary, 132
focus on the, 9
great, 8, 16, 20, 62, 76, 171, 172, 177
guide and inspire team members, 2
hard driving and charismatic, 62
help us become our best selves, 16–17
ignore fundamental human principles, 2
incorrect prototype of, 62
most outstanding, 8
need to let go, 10
need to listen to dissenters, 110
perspective, 14
responsibility, 10
shift from me to team begins with the, 10, 13
leadership/leadership's,
authoritarian, 9
challenge, 2
control, 9
control, authority, expertise, and, 8–9
on the front, 8–9
of the future, 18, 159–175
Guiding Principles and, 59
influence of officers coming from WWII on, 8
job, 59
and listening, 82–83
me, 9
responsibilities, 16
role in encouraging bottom-up alignment, 129–130
sensitivity to feelings, 59–60
shift from Me to Team, 8–9, 10, 13
stories, 25

team, 9
team-focused, 9
"top-down," 9
learning, 57
    from clients, 177
    from each other, 173
    and growing, 24, 39, 72, 120, 131,
        172–173
    growing, and competing, 42, 45–47,
        100, 106, 163
    growing, and teaching, 57
    organization, 75, 173
    organizations that value, 136
    See also four stages of development
learnings, most important for author, 22
let go, need to, 10
life,
    begins to flow more effortlessly, 14
    -defining stories, 32
    fulfilled, meaningful, 41
    home, 2
    intentional and purposeful, 42
    journey, 17
    jungle of, 11, 15, 16, 21, 32
    in service, 47
    true to our purpose and vision, 41
    our best, 16
    work, 2
lives,
    organization positively impacts
        people's, 17
    our motivations and our, 43
    richer, 17
    roles organizations play in creating
        better, 18
London, 52
love, 31, 57, 60, 63, 164, 169
loyalty, 57

M
maturity, 44, 47, 51, 52, 75, 79, 100,
    163 165, 167
MBA, 26
McMillan, Don, 41
me to team,
    journey, 22
    shift from, 8–9, 10, 13, 36, 48
meaning,
    of foundational stories, 21
    lack of, 14
media, electronic, 53
medical professionals, 49
mentor(s), 30, 41, 48
mentoring, 57, 79, 173
metrics,
    of alignment, 107
    departments' operating, 127
    indicators of Peak Performance, 127
    for individual, department, and
        organizational responsibility,
        126–127
    Job Competency Fit and objective,
        119
    and job satisfaction, 161
    key leadership, 173
    Key Objective, 127
    leadership too focused on, 110
    linked to Purpose, Vision, and
        Guiding Principles, 126
    to measure organizational success,
        122
    Objective Key, (OKM), 126, 180
    Organizational Key, 126
    Peak Performance gap and, 173
    regular review of key, 147
    that shares progress toward the
        Vision Objective, 150, 157

of success, 149
successful Peak Performance and,
    120
for team member effectiveness, 122
updates on, 152
Michigan Athletics, 8, 29, 61, 137
Michigan Football, 5, 8, 24, 27, 28,
    124, 137, 156
Michigan State, 104, 105
middle age, 51
money, 46, 78, 115, 155, 156, 162, 163
morale, 56, 123
mortgage industry, 46
motivation(s),
    behind what you are doing, 43
    Four Stages of Fulfillment and,
        41–52
    of workforce, 25
    and our energy, 43

N
NBA Detroit Pistons, 140
NCAA, 63, 64, 105
needs,
    and desires, 41
    immediate, 45
    primary physical, 42, 43–45
    See also four stages of development
Nehlen, Don, 27
New Jersey,
New York City, 26
New York Giants, 25
newspaper industry, 53–54

O
Objective Key Metric (OKM), 126, 180
obstacles, 24
Ohio State Buckeyes, 5–8
openness, 57, 84, 179

operating practices, 58, 106
operating systems, 123,
orders, giving, 9
organization/organization's
    generative,
    greatness, 22
    honoring the, 18
    journey, 22
    Peak Performance and Core Iden-
        tity, 15
    power of sharing energizing stories
        for, 32
    purpose and principles, 32
    stated shared purpose for, 38
    Vision, 18
Organizational Culture Fit, 86, 109,
    111, 117, 118, 119, 120, 124, 126,
    141, 181
oxytocin, 13, 42, 48, 58, 77, 86

P
parent(s), 49, 159
partnering, 13
passion, 9
    for the work, 16
    to serve others, 71, 75, 81, 96
Peak Performance, 8, 10, 38
    360° assessments and, 125–126
    achieving, 56
    aligning the organization to, 137
    alignment to, 66
    assessment template, 180–183
    becoming the standard, 84
    behaviors, 142
    best knowledge available and, 173
    clarity about, 94
    confusion about, 85
    Core Identity, 99, 119, 141, 142
    critical factors for sustainable, 117

culture, 68, 74, 84, 99, 114, 121, 135, 162
desired picture of, 131
disciplines that institutionalize, 99
enablers of, 117–121
energy for, 58
equation, 118, 120
evaluation, 120–121
gap(s), 121, 129, 130, 138, 140, 141, 142, 148, 159, 161, 170, 173
job behavior fit and, 117, 120
job competency fit and, 119–120
journey to, 121, 124, 126
how members achieve, 56
new standards for our own, 121
organization's, 36
organizational culture fit and, 117, 118–119
perspectives and, 171
reinforcing systems and, 101–113, 142
requires new purposeful habits, 97
seeking, 96
shift from me to team and, 10, 177
standard, 122
stories of, 66, 84, 86, 91
stress blockers and, 58
sustainable, 17, 117, 124, 137
for sustainable success, 127
systems that institutionalize, 99
team's journey to, 74, 75
team members' commitment to, 132
team members positioned for, 59
for team success, 139
understanding, 174, 175
what your team is feeling and, 60
working from home and, 80
Penn State, 59
performance,
    optimal, 5

peak, 8, 10
Performance Gap, 121–129, 137, 141, 170, 173–174, 175
perks, 1135
persistence, 57
person we are meant to be, 21
perspective(s),
    collective, 11
    diverse, 13
    limitations of our, 16
    not being open to another's, 12
    our, 11–12
Plato, 3
Porras, Jerry, 28
positivity, 16, 57, 60, 120, 184
possibility of becoming more, 16
potential,
    human, 25
    significant, 17
powerlessness, feeling of, 14
President Ford, 73
pressure,
    Guiding Principles and, 58
    how we respond under, 58
    knowing what to say when under, 12–13, 25
prestige, 46, 47, 89
principles,
    alignment with our shared, 58
    guiding. See Guiding Principles
    our, 32
    timeless, 2–3
    violated, 58
problems,
    recurring, 2
productivity, innovative, 9
professional/professionalism, 57, 60
promotions/titles, 135
Providence, Rhode Island, 26

Purpose, 15, 18, 25–26, 88, 91, 154. *See also* Core Identity
  alignment, 111, 117, 156, 181
  that benefits others, 51
  clear, 90, 179
  compelling, 38–40, 118, 161
  connection to our life's, 42
  consequences of lacking a clear, 156
  that contributes to benefit of others, 48
  Core Identity and, 70, 91, 100, 113, 117, 118, 160
  Culture Clarification and, 92, 99
  daily to-do's and, 157
  deep and meaningful shared, 18
  definition of, 89
  energizes, 90
  energizing, 137
  examples from clients, 89–90
  gratifying, 161
  greater, 177
  and Guiding Principles, 50, 80
  honoring, 41
  leadership's core, 173–174
  life's, 42
  meaningful, 56, 90
  metrics linked to, 127
  organization's energizing, 36
  organization's strengths and capabilities and, 86
  Organizational Culture Fit and, 120
  Patagonia's, 76, 155
  Peak Performance Core Identity and, 111
  powerful and meaningful, 32
  referencing our, 66
  revealed in Culture Clarification process, 89
  revealing the organization's shared, 89–90
  that serves others, 62
  service-oriented, 50, 62
  serving a higher, 162–165
  shared, 140
  significant, 161
  stated shared, 38
  statement, 42
  survey to reveal components of, 70
  sustainable, 49
  sustainable success and, 35
  for team, 140
  team-oriented, 109
  Vision and, 54
  voting for deciding components of, 68
  work in service of, 90

Q
questioning, 24
questions, asking, 9

R
recession, 46
reflection, 24
Reinforcing Systems, 65
  better habits and, 18
  caring and, 102
  confusing and counterproductive, 109
  Core Identity and, 101, 109, 130
  definition of, 36
  disciplined, 109
  Dynamic Strategic Planning and, 146
  effectiveness of disciplined, 103
  flow for sustainable success and, 129
  lack of necessary, 38
  leadership and, 142
  me orientation and, 109

misaligned with Values, 109
new habits and, 84, 96
Organizational Culture Fit and, 86
Peak Performance and, 142
Peak Performance culture and, 84
as practices that reinforce the Core
    Identity, 36
standards and, 96, 109
support Peak Performance, 101–113
support teamwork, 100
transformative change and, 103
relationship,
    boundaries, 57
    builders, 171
    building, 171
    lasting, 60
    bet/ leader and team, 82
    great, 77
    management, 171
    personal, 121
    trust and caring in, 60
reliable/reliability, 57
remote work, 159
resilient/resilience, 57, 60
resources, providing, 23
respect, 11, 40, 57, 60, 63, 68, 83, 84,
    89, 95, 96, 110, 112, 154, 160, 161,
    166, 168–169, 174, 177
responsibility, 57, 114
    for alignment with Core Identity,
        141
    of all organization members, 68
    to be the best we can, 11
    bigger than each individual, 7
    for caring about others, 113
    to consistently reinforce boundar-
        ies, 65
    for creating flow, 131
    credibility and, 60

for culture alignment, 131
for decision-making, shared,
    131–132
disciplined, 15, 141
to energize the team, 10
final, 30
high-potential people and greater, 130
honesty, integrity, and, 60
to honor organization's Peak Perfor-
    mance culture, 68
to honor tradition, 7
individual to collective, 95
leaders', 159, 170. 174
leadership's, 65, 95, 105, 129
maturity and, 79
for modeling expected behavior, 106
for one's own life, 137
organizational, 126
for organizational alignment, 117
to others, 126–129, 173
more profound, 7
social, 76
sustainable success and, 131
taking, 62
trust and, 60
to unleash the dormant greatness,
    13
for welfare of others, 47
responsiveness, 57
results,
    extraordinary, 9
    positive and predictable, 20
reticular activating system (RAS),
    54–55, 56, 148–149. *See also*
    Dynamic Strategic Planning
rewards, 10, 57
Reward and Recognition Committee, 113
Richardson, Jim, 63, 139

right and wrong, feeling of, 11, 21, 33, 39, 43
Robinson, Rumeal, 59
Rose Bowl, 6
rules,
  counterproductive, 24
  respect for, 24

S

sacrifices, 42
sadness, 58
safety and security,
  doing the right things and, 42
  long-term, 18, 19
  for our community, 39, 41, 50
Schembechler, Bo, 6, 24, 27–28
scoreboard, 127
Scott Paper Company, 22
Seiko, 53
self,
  becoming one's best, 22
  best, 14
  -discovery, 22
  -esteem, 12
  -interest, 50
selfishness, 50
serotonin, 42, 48, 58, 77, 86
serving others, 22–23, 50
Shkreli, Martin, 46
Sinek, Simon, 39
skepticism, 13
skills, 15, 47, 75, 147, 182,
Socrates, 3
Southwest Airlines, 61
Spitzer, Fr. Robert, 41
St. Paul's Cathedral, 52
Stage I of Organizational Flow, 37, 42, 43–45, 163

Stage II of Organizational Flow, 38, 42, 45–47, 48, 50, 52, 100, 106, 163
Stage III of Organizational Flow, 38, 42, 47–50, 51, 77, 105, 163, 165, 173
Stage IV of Organizational Flow, 38, 42, 50, 51–52, 163
Stage V of Organizational Flow, 38
standards,
  high, 7, 25
  for working together, 56
Stanford, 64
Start with Why, 39
status, 46,
  of initiatives, 150, 152, 157
  of deliverable, 147
status quo, 68
stories,
  on author's journey, 22–32
  capitalizing on, 32
  de-energizing, 32
  energizing, 32
  foundational, 21
  illuminating, 17
  journaling and, 32
  life-defining, 32
  life-impacting, 22
  organizations', of performing at its best, 17
  that reveal our foundation, 17, 21–33
  reveal our natural strengths, 32
  reveal the person we are today, 21, 32, 33
  role of foundational, 32
  shape who individuals become, 17, 32
  that exemplify transformation, 19
  that impact your life, 32

of those we do not admire, 32
storytelling,
    behaviors and, 64
    feelings and, 86
    Guiding Principles and, 65
    key role of, 86–90
    natural greatness of organizations
        and, 22
strategy, 13
strengths,
    stories reveal our natural, 32
stress/stressed, 123
    blockers, 42, 58
    de-energized and, 19
    de-energizing, 9
    extraordinary, 16
    hormones, 13, 42, 58
    inside the organization, 154
    operational, 157
    on our physiology, 12
    relieve the, 59
    response, 13
    that shortens lives, 9
    team members, 14
stress-cycle of doing, 43
struggles, 21
success,
    consistent, 8
    creating sustainable, 33
    enablers of, 28, 35, 39
    flow for sustainable, 38
    foundation for sustainable, 15
    greatness that resides in each, 19
    individual, 9
    is about people, 25
    is a process, 23
    journey to sustainable, 32
    long-term sustainable, 8, 18

natural, 3
    recipe for sustainable, 28–29
    reinforcing sustainable, 18, 36,
        99–142
    short-term, 41
    systematization of, 8
    sustainable, 3, 17, 18, 28–29, 32, 38,
        48, 99–142
    sustainable flow for, 37
    team, 9
sustainability,
    how to create, 29
    successful, 40
Sutherland, Bob, 40, 41
Swiss watchmakers, 53
systems,
    disciplined, 33
    reinforcing, 18, 36, 38

T
talents, 15, 16
    collective, 9
    individual unique set of, 11, 15
Taylor, Billy, 6–7
team(s)/teams',
    aligning habits for the, 107
    alignment, 134, 141
    are struggling, 1–3
    becoming better, 77
    building, 30
    -centered mindset, 160
    collegiate athletic, 101
    comfort zone, 136
    Core Identity and, 95, 141
    culture, 107, 141
    culture fit and, 174
    diverse, 112
    effectiveness, 123
    engagement process, 70

exceptional leaders and, 168
extraordinary, 179–180
feedback and, 134
-focused approach, 48
giving power to the, 12
Guiding Principles and the, 88
growth, 74
identity, 105
impact of giving power to the, 83
intrinsic stability of your, 172
leadership, 68, 70, 132, 153, 170
loyal, 75
management, 72
maturity, 100
me mindset and, 103
members, dormant greatness in
    each, 13
most outstanding, 8
organizational alignment and, 117
-oriented model, 132
-oriented Purpose, 109
Peak Performance and, 75, 85
Peak Performance Core Identity
    and, 119, 142
peak-performing, 101
performance, 89
perspective, 50
positive energy in, 71
potential, 58
Reinforcing Systems and, 96
with a shared vision, 9
shared Purpose, 10, 18
shift from me to, 95, 99, 101, 116, 131,
    138, 139, 162, 168, 173, 177
standards, 105
strategy or science behind excep-
    tional, 8
success, 105, 111, 129, 139
for sustainable success, 104

sustainably successful, 117
think like a, 138
Vision, 18
team builder, 30
team members/members',
    aligned, 161
    alignment, 84, 130, 134
    assessing, 107, 124–129
    better lives for, 154
    caring and, 102, 171
    committee responsibilities, 130
    commitment and fulfillment, 166
    compelling Vision and, 148
    Competency Fit, 120
    confusing actions and, 148
    Core Identity and, 35, 85, 91–93,
        111, 114, 118
    Culture Clarification interviews
        and, 110
    Culture Fit and, 120
    decision-making and, 116, 131
    deep caring for, 71, 78–81, 97, 167,
        172, 175
    developing, 164
    disruptive, 100
    who don't choose to grow, 86
    Dynamic Strategic Planning and, 146
    effective leaders and, 170
    effective systems and, 122
    effectiveness, 123
    emotional stories and, 152
    emotionally engaging, 160
    emulating leaders, 129
    enabling, to thrive, 17
    Essential Success Factors and, 113
    exemplary performance, 113
    failing or struggling, 174
    feedback, 118
    feel heard and respected, 72

feelings of safety and security and, 110

Foundation of Greatness in each, 19, 177

future, 175

of the future, 162, 169

gap on Peak Performance, 138, 140, 173

giving credit to the, 174

growth opportunities and, 173

hurt or upset, 88

individual greatness of each, 20

Job Competency Fit and, 119

journey, 22

leaders that can be trusted and, 77

leaders who care for, 164

lens through which, view the organization, 86

lives, 82

metrics for effectiveness, 122

motivations, 152

needs, 167

organization's future and, 132

and Organizational Culture Fit, 109, 111

Peak Performance and, 132, 139, 180

Peak Performance evaluation, 120

performance gap and, 137, 141, 148, 161

performance reviews and, 118

perspectives, 19, 83

Purpose, 90

reacting under pressure, 87

Reinforcing Systems and, 109

remote work and, 159

respecting, 171

right, 17

sharing stories, 86, 87, 89, 95

shift from me to team, 111

success and failure, 17

trust, 113

uninspired, dysfunctional, or combative, 14

view of leader, 95

Vision of a better future, 145

younger, 169

team sports, 23

teamwork, 56, 57, 58, 60

testimonials, that exemplify transformation, 19

thinking,
    purposefully, 54
    strategically, 39, 54

to-do list, 43, 55

top-ten life to-do's, 55, 56

training and coaching, 16

transformation,
    is possible, 19
    stories of, 17

transparency, 57

triumphs, 21

trust, 11, 13, 56, 57, 60, 61–63, 64, 68, 69, 71, 77, 83, 89, 95, 96, 97, 110, 112, 113, 125, 135, 159, 160, 167, 168, 175, 186

Turing Pharmaceuticals, 46

U

underperformance, 16

University of Michigan, 5–8, 24, 27, 63, 139, 156, 183, 186

Unleashing Your Foundation of Greatness retreat, 43

V

values,
    that are being honored, 30
    important for author, 22

Vision(s), 15, 18, 30–31, 154, 156
  alignment, 111, 181
  articulate the, 144
  become reality, how, 54–56
  of a better future/tomorrow, 39,
    100, 140, 146
  compelling, 38–40, 107, 113, 141,
    144, 145, 147, 148, 157
  components of, 70
  confidence in, 141
  that contributes to a better future, 51
  Core Identity and, 70, 91, 99, 100,
    113, 117, 118, 160
  daily to-do's and, 157
  of a desired future, 54
  dynamic shift in, 155
  everything we do should be in ser-
    vice of our, 52–53
  followers because of, 155
  gap bet/ where you are and, 141,
    148, 157
  honoring, 41
  initiatives to close gaps, 150
  that impacts your life, 30
  inspirational, 56
  inspiring, 52, 53, 118
  journey toward, 96, 122, 148, 149
  knowledge required to reach, 147
  living life with faith in a, 51
  metrics linked to, 127
  motivating, 31, 32
  objectives, 145, 147, 149–151, 157
  organization's, 18, 36, 52
  organizational actions and the, 148
  organizational Culture Fit and, 111,
    120
  path to the, 148
  power of a positive, 55
  Purpose and, 127, 156
  shared, 9, 18, 52, 138, 144, 147
  start with your, 145
  statement, 31
  strategically plan the, 93
  sustainable success and, 35
  of what we hope to attain, 143
  for your life, 51
vulnerability, 14

W
Weinzweig, Ari, 48
Whetten, David, 61
who we are,
  journaling and, 32
  stories reveal, 22, 32, 33
  understanding, 21
who we are meant to be, 21
  components of, 32
  stories reveal, 22
who we could become, 23
wisdom, 13
Wolverine, 24
work,
  ethic, 22
  impactful on society,
  life, 2
  how we are meant to, together, 17
  real purpose of our daily, 18
  as series of quid pro quo arrange-
    ments, 50
  volunteer, 49
workforce,
  energy level of, 25
  motivation of, 25
Wren, Christopher, 52
WWII, 8

Z
Zingerman's Family of Business, 48

Made in the USA
Columbia, SC
14 January 2025

51792661R00128